Children's Missionary Library

by
Vernon Howard
and
Alice Bostrom

 ACCELERATED CHRISTIAN EDUCATION
Ministries Reaching the World for Christ—One Child at a Time™

Lewisville, Texas

David Livingstone
©1982 Impact Life, DBA Bible Memory Association.

ACCELERATED CHRISTIAN EDUCATION
P.O. Box 299000
Lewisville, Texas 75029-9000

©1998 Accelerated Christian Education,® Inc.

ISBN 1-56265-063-7

3 4 5 6 7 Printing/Year 06 05 04 03 02

Printed in the United States of America

TABLE OF CONTENTS

Book   Page

1. Hudson Taylor
   of the China Inland Mission.................. 5

2. Wilfred Grenfell
   Adventurer to the North 29

3. David Brainerd
   Trailblazer to the Indians........................ 55

4. John G. Paton
   Missionary to the South Seas................ 77

5. Ann Judson
   Friend of Burma...................................... 101

6. Pandita Ramabai
   Heroine of India 123

7. David Livingstone
   Missionary to Africa............................... 149

NOTE: These missionary biographies were originally
       published as separate books. They have now
       been combined into one volume titled *Children's
       Missionary Library*.

HUDSON TAYLOR
OF THE CHINA INLAND MISSION

Story by Vernon Howard

A THRILLING STORY

One afternoon an English lad named James Hudson Taylor wandered into the library of his Yorkshire home. Being a lively boy, his eyes sought a book with a throbbing title. After searching among the books for a few minutes, he came across a Gospel tract.

"These little tracts sometimes have stories at the beginning," he told himself. "I'll just read the story and skip the sermon part."

Almost without realizing it, he finished the story and kept on reading. With mounting interest, he settled himself to read the Gospel message. What an exciting story it was, he admitted. Why, the Man of Galilee had willingly laid down His life so an entire world might have everlasting life! Conviction gripped his soul, and Hudson accepted Jesus as his Saviour.

A strange thought entered his mind. Here was a story that everyone—everyone in the world—should know. And this meant that someone had to tell them. Hudson Taylor knew that there were faraway places all over the world where the people had never read the Bible.

Now that he was a Christian, wasn't it up to him to tell the story? It seemed likely! He then began to wonder where he should go. To what part of the globe should he take the Gospel?

THE ANSWER

To what country should he go as a missionary? To Arabia, that rugged land of fiery deserts and fast-riding horsemen? To India, or to Africa, or perhaps to some lonely island of the South Seas?

Young Hudson did not wonder for long, for he soon came across a book entitled *China*. His heart began to thump madly. What thrilling stories he had read about *this* mysterious land on the other side of the globe. This was the empire of peculiar temples and idols, dedicated to the false teachings of Buddha.

He knew that China's desperate millions needed the Gospel. "Poor, neglected China," he told his sister. "Scarcely anyone cares about it." But did God want him to go to China?

He earnestly prayed about it. Before long, the answer came clearly to the young Christian:

"Then go for Me to China."

He would prepare now! Securing a Gospel of Luke in Chinese, he set it alongside his English Bible. By carefully comparing Chinese with English, he was soon able to read simple sentences. He also studied medicine, knowing that he must be a doctor as well as a missionary to the Chinese people. "That land is ever in my thoughts," he told his sister as he made himself ready for the Orient.

"THE WIND IS COMING!"

Hudson finally caught the ship *Dumfries*, bound for Shanghai. Like most voyages of the day, it was a perilous one of squalls and battering seas. A strange and wonderful incident occurred while they were off the coast of New Guinea. The *Dumfries* suddenly found itself without wind in its sails, helplessly drifting toward the rocks of the nearby shore. The captain gloomily turned to Hudson and spoke.

"Well, we have done everything that can be done. We can only await the result."

"No, there is one thing we have not done yet," Taylor cheerfully replied.

"What is that?" asked the captain.

"Four of us on board are Christians," replied the young missionary. "Let us each retire to his cabin and in agreed prayer ask the Lord to give us immediately a breeze."

As the captain nodded, Hudson withdrew and prayed for a wind. He then asked the skeptical first mate to let down the sail. To the amazement of everyone but the four Christians, the sail began to tremble before a swelling breeze.

"The wind is coming!" the happy first mate shouted, and minutes later the *Dumfries* once more began to nudge its way toward the China coast.

A WARM WELCOME!

No sooner had Hudson stepped off the boat than he found himself caught in the midst of Chinese wars. It seemed as if he had landed on an unsettled island, shaking beneath his feet. So fierce was the fighting in Shanghai that his life was threatened several times within the first few days. Deep-throated cannons rocked the city all day long, while angry bullets shattered windows of the mission itself.

"We walked some distance round the wall," he wrote, "and sad it was to see the wreck of rows upon rows of houses near the city. Burnt down, blown down, battered to pieces— in all stages of ruin they were!"

A fainter heart than Hudson's might have been tempted to take the first ship back to England. But he knew that God wanted him *here*. There would be no retreating for this warrior. Arming himself with books and tracts, he boldly marched through Shanghai. Since there was fighting to be done, he would get into it! After all, he was a soldier of the Cross.

Knowing that his life was always in danger, he wrote, "If you hear of my being killed or injured, do not think it a pity that I came, but thank God I was permitted to distribute some Scriptures and tracts for Him Who died for me."

A STRANGE PULPIT

Inland China! It was young Taylor's fervent hope from the beginning that he might carry the Gospel to the multitudes of the unreached interior. He soon set about making his first journey to the inland regions. Teaming up with another young missionary, he rented a houseboat and nosed it into the rough waters of the Yangtze River.

He did not have to search out adventure, for it rushed to his side in a maze of thrilling incidents. The great river looked to him like a tremendous serpent crawling through the country. Teeming masses of folks spent their entire lives on its waters.

On one occasion Taylor moored his boat to the island of Yen-yu Leo, intending to preach to the islanders. Hearing chatter at his back that sounded like firecrackers, he was startled to see hundreds of curious natives from the mainland crowding across the water toward them. Like a swarm of friendly bees, they soon surrounded the missionaries. To keep from being mobbed, Taylor reboarded his boat and pushed away from the island. With cheerful shouts, the eager Chinese splashed into the water after him.

With a deck as a pulpit, Hudson spent the afternoon telling his wet listeners of God's love for them.

THE MANDARIN GIVES AN ORDER

One day Hudson and another missionary were passing out tracts in the dangerous city of Tung-chow. They suddenly found themselves surrounded by a band of soldiers, led by a tall, powerful officer. Hudson wrote of the attack, "He all but knocked me down again and again, seized me by the hair, took hold of my collar so as almost to choke me, and grasped my arms and shoulders, making them black and blue."

They were eventually hauled before the mandarin who ruled Tung-chow. His name was Ch'en Ta Lao-ie. Taylor immediately pulled out his books and began to preach the Gospel. The mandarin listened politely and thanked Hudson for the books. Then, to the surprise of everyone, especially Hudson, Ch'en Ta Lao-ie clapped his hands, which brought servants loaded with refreshments. He invited the missionaries to join him in food and drink.

When Hudson and his friend were ready to leave, the mandarin gave strict orders that the Christians were not to be harmed in any way. Also, they could preach whenever and wherever they liked.

Gathering up his remaining books, Hudson boldly marched through the center of the baffled mob outside the palace. The adventure was safely ended, although there were many, many more to come!

A CHANGE OF CLOTHES!

Hudson had not been in China very long before he began to notice something strange. Whenever he stood up to preach, many of the Chinese seemed to be staring curiously at him, instead of giving full attention to his words. Every now and then, some of the boys and girls would grin and point at him. Perhaps some of them even whispered loud enough for him to hear.

Ch'i kwai!

He knew this meant, "How odd!" But what did they mean? He was certainly not

an odd-looking man. Then it struck him. His clothes! They were amused at his appearance. To the Chinese, his European dress was quite comical. Perhaps they asked themselves why this white missionary wore such awkward clothing, when Chinese dress was far more fitting to the Chinese climate.

Taylor began to wonder. Why not adopt the Chinese dress? It would help his listeners to concentrate on his message instead of on his clothes. He would do it!

He was instantly delighted with the results, for he discovered that he was now accepted as one of their own. Chinese hearts and homes were open to him as never before.

AI-IA! CH'I KWAI!

Years swiftly passed as Taylor plunged headlong into his work. One of his most important activities was the hospital at Shanghai. With medicine in one hand and a Bible in the other, he went among his patients.

"O shin! Jesu chui liao o!" they would shout, "I believe! Jesus saved me!"

When he was able to get away from the hospital, Hudson gathered supplies and began a tireless trudge among the villages of the interior. Whenever he entered a settlement for the first time, it was as if he had come with a stick of burning dynamite in his hand. Like stampeding cattle, the natives scrambled away. *Who*—and *what*—was this strange creature with the "Jesus" books?

"Ai-ia! Ch'i kwai! Oh, how strange!" they screamed, darting to the safety of their homes. Hudson wrote of his experiences near the city of Huang-king:

"When I first entered the town, people ran away as from a wild animal! At first the people were frightened, but this soon wore off. . . . Set off early this morning with books, and spent the whole day going from house, hamlet, and village. . . . Many persons followed us, wanting medicines, either for themselves or their friends. . . . I told them of Jesus."

A MISSION IS BORN!

A strange thing suddenly happened to Hudson Taylor. He found that he must leave

China. It was impossible—yet true! His health had suffered during these first few years. He knew there was only one thing to do. He must return to England for a rest.

Was this the end of his adventures in China? Hudson did not know it, but it was just the beginning!

Back in England, he began to ask himself many questions. What could be done for the millions of neglected Chinese far in the interior of the empire? Thousands of tiny villages were untouched by the Gospel. How could he reach these people of *inland China*?

While walking one day along the sands of Brighton Beach, an idea struck him. Why not establish a mission whose purpose would be to reach these villages far inland from the coast? Again, he knew that God was leading him. Again, he began to visualize China, but this time it was the rolling hills and hidden valleys of inland China. His heart began to race with excitement. He would begin a new work for these faraway natives. And what should he call this new mission? He had it!

THE CHINA INLAND MISSION!

THE ANSWER MAN!

Returning to China, Taylor again thrust himself into the interior. Wherever he went, he found an intense curiosity on the part of the natives who gathered around him. They were eager to hear the words of this Englishman who spoke the Chinese tongue and preached about a man from Galilee. What sort of a man was this Christian missionary? they asked themselves. *What* did he preach, *why* did he preach, and *how* could it help them? Whenever Hudson said something that was not clear, they boldly spoke up.

"What does the Christian God look like?"

"Did Jesus die for everyone in China?"

"Why do you say our idols are useless?"

He sometimes shocked his listeners by preaching in front of the Buddhist shrines or idol-filled pagodas. One time, in order to tower over his audience, he clambered upon a bronze incense vase in a temple entrance. The Buddhist priests stood silently by to hear him.

Many times he found more than a thousand interested Chinese before him, but he never tired of answering their questions. Perhaps he realized that many who stood before him today would not return on the morrow.

"*Puh ts'o! Puh ts'o!* Not wrong! Not wrong!" they would shout as they agreed with his words.

"WHAT DO YOU WANT?"

Ch'iang tao! Ch'iang tao!
This is a dreadful cry for the traveler in China to hear, for it means, "Robber! Robber!" One night, Hudson Taylor cleverly outwitted three thieves.

Weary from a long day's journey, he sat down against the wall of a temple. Hearing the stealthy shuffling of padded feet, he raised his head to see shadowy figures creeping toward him. He spoke sharply into the darkness.

"What do you want?"

Seeing that the missionary was not asleep, the robbers hesitated. "You had better lie down and sleep," one of them replied. "Otherwise, you will be unable to work tomorrow."

Hudson was not deceived. "Listen to me," he commanded. "I know what you are and what you intend to do." He told them that he trusted God to protect him. By singing hymns and repeating Bible verses, he managed to keep his head from nodding.

"Do not be mistaken," he warned them several times during the night. "I am not asleep."

The robbers finally became discouraged and drifted away, leaving Taylor to close his eyes in badly needed slumber.

THE PROMISED LAND!

Hudson Taylor was always glad to spend a day of rest in the Chinese countryside, gathering specimens of flowers and insects. He wrote of his wanderings in the field:

"I caught sight of a large black butterfly with swallow-tail wings, the largest living butterfly I have ever seen. . . . It nearly took my breath away, it was so fine! There are also wild flowers that are new to me and very pretty."

While hiking between mountain villages, he often paused to admire the beautiful scenery.

Said he, ". . . shades of foliage, from the deep, gloomy cypress to the light, graceful willow, mingled with orange, tallow, and other trees, gave a lively and interesting variety to the scene . . . the brilliant sunlight threw an air of gladness over everything."

A startling thought came to Hudson as he gazed over the colorful valleys and hills. China belonged to *him*. It was true! God had given China to him as his Promised Land. It was his for the sake of the Gospel. Again, he wrote his appreciation of the view:

"The country below, covered with early crops and tended like a garden, was of the brightest hue, owing to recent rains. . . . Several little lakes shining like molten silver put a finishing touch to the beauty of the scene."

THE BOXERS STRIKE!

The China Inland Mission was now spreading out like the spokes of a wheel. Like flaming torches in the night, new missionaries were plunging into the heart of China with the Gospel story.

Hudson himself was traveling all over the globe, telling Christian men and women of China's great need. He reminded them that almost four hundred million Chinese were without the Gospel. Among other countries, he visited the United States, Canada, New Zealand, Australia, and Sweden.

Though the work of the China Inland Mission was growing larger, it was by no means easier. During one of Taylor's trips away from China, the terrible Boxer Rebellion struck the country. The Boxers were angry Chinese who wanted to drive all foreigners from China's soil. Screaming mobs of Boxers swarmed through the streets, attacking Christians and destroying mission property.

It seemed as if almost overnight the work of Hudson Taylor and his friends would be swept away. But Hudson knew that it was also God's work. With the Lord's help, they would send forth other missionaries to build new stations.

"I love the Chinese more than ever," he once wrote. "Oh, to be useful among them!"

"HOW PRETTY YOU ARE!"

"What beautiful white skins you have!"

This was the exclamation of Chinese women who saw lady missionaries for the first time. Their eyes wide with curiosity, the Chinese women crowded around the English ladies. Chattering happily, they ran their hands up and down the European clothing, grasped the missionaries' hands, and patted their cheeks.

"You are so beautiful," they said to the embarrassed ladies, "and as fresh as early almond blossoms. But why have you come to this country? What is in those little baskets you carry?"

This gave the missionaries an opportunity to pass out Gospel literature and speak for Christ. And when they sang hymns in Chinese, the native women responded with cries of delight.

Taylor knew how important the missionary wives and daughters were to their menfolk. He was deeply grateful for his own wife Maria, for it was her prayers and patience that helped him through the early years of his Chinese work. Maria Taylor helped in the hospital,

taught at the missionary school, and worked constantly at her husband's side.

"We want a missionary of our own," a group of Chinese women once told Taylor, "and we want a *lady!*"

"DEAR AND VENERABLE PASTOR"

It was now more than fifty-one years since the young Hudson Taylor had first set foot on Chinese soil. He had seen the China Inland Mission expand into a network of mission stations all over the empire. Thousands of Chinese Christians were now working alongside the foreign missionaries. Millions of Bibles, books, and tracts were getting into the hands of the needy people.

Taylor was resting in Switzerland when he saw that life was drawing to a close. Deciding on one more trip to his beloved China, he landed on the coast of Shanghai, the same city he had first entered fifty-one years before.

Like a victorious but humble soldier, he visited the various mission stations, including several along the familiar Yangtze River. It was the last the Chinese were to see of their

"Dear and Venerable Pastor" here on Earth. But they would never forget this heroic man who had given a lifetime of service for them. The thrilling Gospel story he had first understood in his Yorkshire home was now *their* story too.

"Had I a thousand lives," he once said, "China should claim every one."

WILFRED GRENFELL
ADVENTURER TO THE NORTH

Story by Vernon Howard

"LOOK, WILL!"

If you had lived a number of years ago near the River Dee in England, you might have seen two lively boys poling an awkward craft along the rushing waters of the river. You would have noticed that the boys were probably brothers, for they looked alike. Perhaps you might even have heard them shouting to each other as they struggled against the current.

"Look, Will, over there! That's the longest-legged curlew I ever saw. Let's get a closer look."

The boy called Will was a sturdy youth with laughing eyes. He nodded to his brother and set his pole hard against the river.

"We don't want to scare it away," Will called back. "We want to get just close enough to study it. Remember, we need a whole collection of marsh birds to make our scrapbook complete."

Will's idea of fun and adventure was to roam the marshes and hills near his home of Parkgate. Every expedition meant some new butterfly or bird or flower for his growing collection. His bedroom was jammed with fascinating trophies of his outdoor conquests.

Maybe we should learn more about this happy English lad who spent his boyhood along the sands of Dee. Maybe these youthful adventures are just the beginning of an exciting life. Suppose we follow and see what happened to this boy whose full name was Wilfred Grenfell.

A DECISION

Wilfred made two very important decisions while he was still a young man. He came to the first decision one afternoon when he called upon the family doctor for advice.

"Doctor, I would like to choose an occupation that will be interesting and helpful—and exciting!"

The physician smiled at Wilfred's enthusiasm. "Do you think leaving your home at all hours of the night, rushing to patients' homes in storms and squalls, and having a whole village depending upon you for their very lives could be exciting enough?"

Wilfred carefully thought it over. The life of a doctor was a real adventure, he finally decided. Yes, he would go to medical school at once. And he did.

The second event occurred one evening when Wilfred was on his way home from his studies at a London medical college. He was curiously attracted by a well-lighted hall along the way. He saw posters announcing that two American evangelists were holding Gospel meetings. Something stirred inside the boy's heart. As he remembered his early church training, his conscience bothered him, for he realized he was not living a full Christian life.

He made his second decision at once. He would not only be a doctor, he would be a Christian doctor.

His life was ahead of him. What would he do with it?

TO THE NORTH SEA

By passing all his medical examinations, hard-working Wilfred became known as *Doctor* Grenfell.

"You like the outdoors, Wilfred," a friend told him, "and I know just the place where you can lead a rugged, athletic life."

"Where is that?"

"The fishermen of the North Sea fleets need a doctor. It won't be easy, but it is a splendid opportunity for pioneering. Besides, you will have a chance to preach the Gospel to the men and their families. You see, a Christian mission is sending the man."

Without hesitation, Wilfred accepted the challenge. Almost before he knew it, he was grounded on the bleak coast of the North Sea.

The young physician was caught in a whirlpool of rough-and-ready adventures from the very first. Whether it was braving the fury of a North Sea gale, or working all night to save the life of a fisherman's child, or teaching a Bible class afloat on the high seas, Wilfred never flinched.

Though he did not know it at the time, Dr. Grenfell's labors in the North Sea were part of his schooling for an even greater work.

"You have done a wonderful service for the fishermen," the mission told him. "Now, we want you to pioneer for us in another place—Labrador."

ST. JOHN'S

Labrador! Wilfred's mind leaped to scenes of mountainous icebergs that floated like great white ghosts in misty seas. He thought of cold, dreary wastelands inhabited by Indians and Eskimos, many of them primitive and uncivilized.

"What will be my duties in Labrador?" Grenfell asked.

"That is up to you," he was told. "The mission wants someone to march right in and do whatever is necessary. You must be a doctor, missionary, teacher, carpenter, and an all-around handyman. We believe you can do it."

Going to his map, Dr. Grenfell saw that Labrador was a sprawling wilderness located on the eastern coast of Canada. It was far removed from the civilized centers of both Canada and the United States. But its very isolation and loneliness attracted him.

"I'll go!" he suddenly declared.

He set sail from England a short time later in the *Albert*, a ketch-rigged vessel with a hardy hull. Not many days out, Dr. Grenfell caught sight of his first icebergs. The *Albert* skillfully skirted the icy monsters. Finally they drew near the city of St. John's, in Newfoundland, just south of Labrador. His first sight of the New World was one that foretold his years of high adventure. St. John's was in flames!

PLANS ARE MADE

As much as Dr. Grenfell wished to remain in the destroyed city of St. John's to help the suffering citizens, he knew his duty lay to the north. So the *Albert* once more spread her sails, eventually settling herself in the waters of the Labrador coast.

What kind of a country was this Labrador? What kind of people lived here?

Dr. Grenfell knew that the coastal settlements were populated by Eskimos and a few white folk who struggled with the sea for their livelihood. All summer long they plowed the choppy seas, gathering rich loads of fish

and seals. They worked hard, knowing that, once the blasts of winter fell on them, they must have enough food to last the entire cold season. They were hardened, patient people who suffered a great deal and complained little. The English missionary-doctor determined to share their hardships.

Inland Labrador was a mysterious tangle of white wastes, unexplored except for wandering Indian tribes who spent their days in hunting and trapping. These shy people also needed the medical and spiritual help of Dr. Grenfell.

"The first thing we must do is go among the people and let them know we are here," Wilfred told his assistants. "Let's fix up a smaller boat and scour the coasts."

INVASION OF THE ICEBERGS

To navigate the rugged straits and inlets of the Labrador coast, Dr. Grenfell secured a steam launch, the *Princess May*. The sturdy craft was nosed into the cold seas, and the Labrador invasion was underway. It was a risky voyage from the very first, for the little launch was immediately swallowed by waves of blinding fog.

"The ice packs are like white wolves," the crew gloomily warned as they peered anxiously into the mists. "We'll never know they're on us until it's too late."

"There are uncharted rocks and reefs all about us," an officer remarked. "We'll shatter to splinters if we hit."

Dr. Grenfell was at the helm, watching and praying that they might fight through the dense blanket. His heart leaped in alarm as a shout came from below.

"We've sprung a leak, sir! Shall we make for shore?"

It seemed like a hopeless fight. He was already wandering blindly in slicing seas, not knowing when he would hear the shivering shock of a shattered hull—and now, a leak. Grenfell gripped the wheel all the tighter, thinking of the happy faces he was sure to see when the Eskimos learned he was a doctor, sent to help them.

"Plug it as best you can," he grimly shouted down. "We're not turning back!"

A NEW FRIEND

Courageous Wilfred finally piloted the *Princess May* to the safety of the shore, and the adventure was ended. But other adventures, with Eskimos and Indians, were about to begin. The cabin of the *Princess May* was a haven compared with the outdoor life now before him. Clothing himself in thick furs and arming himself with rifle and knife, Dr. Grenfell plunged into the wilderness in search of the people who needed his services.

"You are a *doctor?*" the Eskimos mumbled in disbelief, as the missionary appeared at the entrance of their igloos. "What are you doing out here in the backwoods? How did you get here?"

Recovering from their surprise, they eagerly invited the missionary-doctor to spend the night beneath their icy roofs. Though the tiny igloos were heavy with the fumes of seal oil lamps and uncomfortably crowded, Wilfred delighted to sit on the floor and talk with his newly made friends. A good part of the evening was spent in doctoring wounds and reading from the Bible.

"It is wonderful to have you with us," the children spoke shyly to the smiling white man. "We do not have many visitors from the big cities of the outside world. Will you please come back very soon?"

"I have hundreds of other igloos to visit," he told them, "but I will not forget to call again."

"OKSUIT!"

The dogsled is as important to a Labrador native as a ship is to a sailor. Dr. Grenfell used his sled—called a *komatik* in Labrador— as both a home and hospital. One afternoon, while Dr. Grenfell was making some calls, a messenger dashed up.

"A boy has been hurt. Come!"

The missionary knew the trip called for every ounce of grit he possessed, for the lad's home was deep in the ice wastes. Anyone else might have been discouraged, but not Wilfred Grenfell. With shouts of "*Oksuit! Oksuit!* Hurry! Hurry!*" he bravely fought his way to the hut of the suffering lad. But now an even greater challenge faced him. He must make the trip to the hospital with his komatik weighted with the helpless boy.

"How far is it to the hospital?" he asked the father.

"About sixty miles."

"What kind of country is it?"

"Very rough, Doctor. The trail leads over rocky hills."

Without hesitation, Wilfred packed the boy in warm furs and placed him in the komatik. Through storms and freezing temperatures, he battled the trail, finally bringing the boy to safety and comfort at the hospital.

WOLF!

"Gypsy, ho! Tiger, come here! Scotty! Spider! Spot! Rover! Shaver! Eric! Tad! This way, boys!"

Had you heard Dr. Grenfell shouting these names some crisp Labrador morning, you might have thought he was calling some of his Eskimo friends to help him prepare for an Arctic journey. Well, he was shouting to friends, but they were all four-footed ones!

These were the huskies of his komatik, often the only companions he had on the icy trails.

These powerful komatik dogs were descendants of the huge Labrador wolves, and they were often as vicious as their wild ancestors. But in spite of primitive instincts, they proved to be faithful and obedient servants who plunged straight into the dangers of the Arctic trails ahead of their master's sled.

"Look!" one of Grenfell's companions shouted one day as he gazed toward the hills. "We have only eight dogs. There are thirteen huskies heading this way."

Another companion peered suspiciously at the thirteen animals as they bounded toward camp. He suddenly raised a rifle to his shoulder.

"Five of them are *not* huskies. They're *wolves.*"

It was true! So wild were the komatik huskies that they had searched out their wild cousins and romped through the hills with them.

ADRIFT!

One April day the missionary received an emergency call from a backwoods hunter who was desperately ill. Dr. Grenfell knew his trip would be a hazardous one, for the winter ice was beginning to break up. A sudden shift in the ice beneath his feet and the mercy doctor might find himself hopelessly adrift in the white seas.

"Be careful of the cracking ice," he was warned by his friends at the base as he prepared to leave. "It is as tricky as an earthquake."

"*Oksuit!* Hurry!" Grenfell called to his eager dogs, and the komatik plummeted down the trail. Half the distance had been covered when it happened—a quick shift in the wind, a sudden sinking of the ice beneath his feet, and Grenfell found himself afloat on a chunk of ice. He prayed quietly, knowing that he was floating out to sea where rescue would be unlikely.

He faced death, but it held no terrors for him. He believed, with the apostle Paul, that

Christ had removed the sting from death, so that for those who trust in Him, death becomes the gateway to Life. The words of an old hymn he had often sung came to his mind:

"My God, my Father, while I stray
Far from my home on life's rough way,
Oh, help me from my heart to say,
'Thy will be done.'"

He tried to make a fire, both to keep warm and to attract attention, if possible; but his matches were too wet. In the bitter cold, he nestled up close to his largest dog and slept a while.

That evening, while four men were fishing, one of them thought he saw something moving on the ice. They hurried to their village and went to the house of a man who owned a small telescope. From the cliffs they could just make out the form of a man drifting on a piece of ice. They guessed that the man was their beloved doctor. At dawn the rescue expedition set out.

Once that morning Dr. Grenfell thought that he saw the glimmer of an oar in the distance, but the bright snow had caused him some snow blindness so that he did not trust his eyesight. At last the boat came nearer, and he could see the rescuers waving wildly.

One of the men jumped onto the ice and shook the doctor's hand. Neither of them spoke a word, as both felt a depth of joy that could not be expressed. Soon the doctor and dogs were aboard the boat on their way to safety.

Dr. Grenfell referred to this incident years later, when he was speaking of the value of memorizing the Scriptures.

"Most gladly I give testimony of my experience concerning the memorizing of Scripture," he said. "To me it has been an unfailing help in doubt, anxiety, sorrow, and all the countless problems of life. I believe in it enough to have devoted many hours to stowing away passages where I can neither leave them behind me nor be unable to get at them.

"Facing death alone on a floating piece of ice on a frozen ocean, the comradeship it afforded me supplied all I needed. With my whole soul I commend to others the giving of some time each day to secure the immense returns Scripture memorization insures."

REINDEER FOR LABRADOR

The energetic Dr. Grenfell was always on the lookout for ways to improve the living standards of his adopted people. He established hospitals, trading posts, an orphanage, and a lumber camp, all of which gave employment to the menfolk. The women were encouraged in basket making and rug weaving.

He gave special thought to providing food all the year around, for many times when fishing and hunting were poor, the Labrador folk were hungry. An inspiration struck him! He spoke to his assistant about it.

"I'm going to import some livestock!"

"Livestock? What kind?"

"Reindeer! And I'm going to send for them at once!"

"*Reindeer?*" was the astonished reply. "Why?"

"Don't you see how valuable they will be?" the missionary-doctor pointed out. "They will always be on hand for food during hard winters. And they can haul loads even better than the huskies."

A short time later, three hundred splendid reindeer arrived from Lapland. Under

Dr. Grenfell's direction, the herd thrived and grew. The Eskimos were delighted with the services of their new animal friends. Especially along the southern parts of the country, where the dogs were less savage and did not harm the animals, the reindeer proved to be a wonderful experiment.

JUDGE AND JURY

The grateful Labrador natives knew Wilfred Grenfell as a skillful doctor, but they also knew him as a missionary. Wherever he journeyed, and whenever he found the opportunity, he preached the Gospel. It was no strange sight to see the energetic Englishman with his medical kit in one hand and his Bible in the other.

The government recognized the wholesome influence of Grenfell and appointed him as district judge. The people were delighted to have the friendly physician as the one who should hold their court and try their legal cases. They knew they were certain to receive justice at his hands.

Grenfell held court wherever he ran into a dispute between neighbors or wherever there was a crime to be punished. His able crew always stood nearby to back up his decisions.

"You have broken the law by robbing another man's traps," a frightened woodsman might hear as Judge Grenfell's accusation. "What do you have to say for yourself?"

"I made a mistake."

"You certainly did; you must be punished." In a kindlier tone, the missionary would add: "I would like to see you at chapel services next Sunday. Will you come?"

"Yes, sir, I will."

FOR POMIUK

"Doctor Grenfell, come at once!"

The missionary snatched up his kit and hurried out. Lying helpless on the shoreline rocks was an Eskimo lad. As his wounds were being bound by the kindly white man, he told a pitiful story.

His name was Pomiuk. Many months before, a party of white men came ashore and told

Pomiuk and his friends of a great country called the United States. They invited some of the families to come with them and visit this wonderful land. Pomiuk and his mother happily accepted and were soon in the great country to the south.

But it was not a happy land for Pomiuk. He was made to wear heavy Arctic clothing all the time, just to show the Americans how the Labrador natives lived. And he was not used to the strange foods and houses the white men provided. To make it even worse, he fell down, injuring his hip.

"I want to go back to my country," he told the white men. "Will you please send me home?"

"It is not always easy to catch a ship to Labrador," he was told. "You will have to wait until one comes along."

After many months of suffering, he finally found a vessel that took him back to his homeland—and final abandonment on the shore.

"I'm going to build an orphanage for boys like Pomiuk!" Dr. Grenfell announced.

SIR WILFRED GRENFELL

As the years passed, Dr. Grenfell's name began to be heard in far corners of the globe. The stories of his mighty work in faraway Labrador were read eagerly by everyone who enjoyed adventure.

"Look!" a Swiss lad might exclaim, "Dr. Grenfell traveled seventy-five miles through a blizzard just to bring medicine to a sick fisherman."

"He has taught the women how to sew and weave and make artificial flowers," a lady of New York might have remarked.

"The king of England is going to knight him," might have been the observation of a London girl.

When King George V touched the mercy doctor on the shoulder with a sword, saying, "Arise, Sir Wilfred Grenfell," it was the world's way of saying "thank you" to the man who had spent his lifetime in humble service to mankind.

If he was a hero to the outside world, Wilfred Grenfell was a magnificent conqueror to his own adopted people. Without swords or guns, he had completely won the country. His only weapons were his devotion, courage, and faith. To the Eskimos and Indians of Labrador, he was their skillful physician, their kindly judge, and their Christian friend.

God had used this man to give them their first schools, their first hospitals, their first orphanages; to teach them farming, trades, and crafts. But most important, God had sent him to tell them of Jesus' love for them, and of His death on Calvary, that "whosoever believeth in Him should not perish, but have everlasting life."

Though he was honored by some of the people of his day, he would not wish us to exalt him for what he did. He wanted his life to exalt the Lord. Perhaps he was such a blessing to others because he learned to trust in the Lord and to say with his whole heart, "Thy will be done."

DAVID BRAINERD
TRAILBLAZER TO THE INDIANS

Story by Vernon Howard

"David, come on! We're hiking to the Indian hills!"

The slender boy whose name had been called shook his head at his friends.

"Not today, Tom. I'd better not go."

"What's the matter, David? Not sick again, are you?"

"No," the boy replied as he sat down on a nearby stump. "I guess I'm just tired."

Young David Brainerd watched regretfully as his friends filed into the woods. He wanted desperately to go with them, but he knew his weak legs could not stand the long hike. He wondered why he should have such a puny body that tired so easily. Why couldn't he have been a hardy pioneer like his Pilgrim ancestors who had settled the state of Connecticut? Why couldn't he have been born with a rugged body that could carry him deep into the Indian hills along with his friends?

David had no answers to his questions. At the time it seemed that he must spend his whole life just sitting on a stump, watching his companions disappear into the trees.

But God had a plan for the New England lad. . . .

THE DECISION

When David grew older, he entered Yale College. He worked hard over his books and soon became an honor student. Still, he was not altogether happy. He longed to be active in Christian work. Shortly after leaving school, he received a letter from a minister in New York. He gasped with delight as he read it.

Dear Mr. Brainerd:

We wish to send a missionary to the New England Indians. We would appreciate your assistance. Can you come to New York at once?

David felt like tossing his clothes into a bag and taking off for New York. But first he would pray about it and talk it over with his friends.

"There is nothing I want more than to preach to the Indians," he told his Christian friends. "But I am not very strong. A missionary to the Indians would have to fight the thick woods and swift streams. It would be a rough life."

"If God wants you to go, He will give you the strength," his friends replied.

It didn't take David any longer to make up his mind. He would go!

A STORMY WAY

When David arrived in New York, he was questioned by the men who had sent for him. Did he really want to spend his life in the lonely woods as a preacher to the Indians?

"I believe God wants me to bring the Gospel to the red men," he answered. "And I will carry on as long as God gives me strength."

Having made up his mind, young David promptly sold his books and extra clothing. Of what use were fancy clothes among the Indians? He had now cut himself off from the world of the white man, and there was only one place where he could be happy. That place was in the forests and valleys where the Indians lived.

David began to write a diary in which he recorded the adventures and experiences that came to him. He wrote of two early hardships:

"I rode all night long through a drenching rain without seeing a single hut or Indian tent. The coldness numbs my fingers so I can scarcely write. . . .

"This morning I came to a raging stream. I do not know how I will get across. I will rest here for a few hours and pray about it. . . ."

A GIFT!

Prayer and hard work solved many problems for the young preacher. But it seemed that no sooner had he licked one problem than another took its place. Among his greatest difficulties were the suspicions of the Indians. Dishonest white traders had cheated the Indians many times before. It was no wonder that they looked upon all white men with distrust.

"I have come to give you the Gospel of Christ," David told them from the very first.

"We think you want our furs," they insisted.

"I am not interested in anything you may have. I want only to tell you of a wonderful gift that God has for you."

A gift! This was something different. What kind of a white man was this?

"Here is a Bible," said David, holding up the Book. "It tells of the Lord Jesus Christ, Who came to Earth many years ago so that all men might have everlasting life. You see, I want to give you something, not take anything away."

"We will listen to you," the Indians agreed, "but you must not try to take our furs."

POWWOWS!

Like most missionaries, David found the uncivilized natives bound by ancient superstitions. He was dismayed to find the Indians worshiping birds, animals, trees, and even the weather. The Indian priests led their people in all sorts of different worship in an effort to please the many gods. The Christian missionary often angered these priests with his pointed questions.

"Why do you worship the wind?" he would ask. "Has it a tongue to speak to you? Has it ears to hear? Can it forgive your sins? Why do you worship the wind?"

Of course, the priests had no reply. They showed their anger by attempting to cast a spell on the missionary. By wild dances and horrible screams, they called down the anger of their gods upon the white man. These priests were called powwows, or magicians.

"You have angered our gods by bringing this strange religion into the forests," the powwows screamed. "The storm wind will carry you into the river or cast you away into the sky!"

David patiently explained that he had no fear of the wind or any of the other strange woodland gods.

THROUGH THE RAPIDS

Since there were many Indian languages and dialects, David often was unable to make himself understood by the Indians. One day he met a young Indian named Tautamy who could speak both English and the Indian tongues.

"I need an interpreter, Tautamy," David told him. "How would you like to go with me on my missionary trips?"

"I am not a preacher, Mr. Brainerd," the Indian youth answered. "I am not even a Christian. I have heard you preach many times, but still I am not a Christian."

"Just the same, I would like to have you with me."

"All right, I'll go."

David and Tautamy traveled the forest trails together. Whenever they came to a tribe whose dialect was unknown to David, he could count on Tautamy to make the Gospel message clear to the natives. David was delighted to have such a faithful and helpful friend. One day, after the missionary had preached a powerful Gospel message, Tautamy came to him.

"Mr. Brainerd, I have just taken Jesus as my Saviour. Now we are *Christian* friends."

DAVID'S DIARY

Much of what we know of the life of David Brainerd comes from the diary he started early in his missionary career. From this day-by-day journal, we learn what incredible hardships this young man went through in order to turn the New England Indians toward the Cross. His diary often reads like an exciting novel of early American days. It is packed with thrilling adventures with hostile Indians and wonderful stories of Indian conversions.

While visiting one village he wrote:

"In the evening they met together, nearly a hundred of them, and danced round a large fire, having prepared ten deer for the sacrifice . . . at the same time yelling and shouting in such a manner that they might easily have been heard two miles or more. They continued their sacred dance all night near the altar. . . . I at length crept into a little crib made for corn and slept on the poles."

Another time he happily wrote:

"The Word of God . . . seemed to fall upon the assembly with a divine power. The dear Christians were refreshed and comforted."

A CLOSE CALL

The journeys of the young missionary were always perilous. To reach some of the remote tribes, he often had to cross steep mountains in the dark of night or pass across treacherous swamps or cut his way through beast-infested forests. It is miraculous that he ever reached some of his destinations alive.

One inky night, David and a companion were attempting to cross a rocky mountaintop. Just below them, hidden in the deep gloom, were sharp gorges.

"Maybe we had better stop for the night," David's companion spoke. "If our horses slip off the rocks, we will plunge hundreds of feet straight down."

Young Brainerd peered into the darkness below. "It would be just as dangerous in the day," he replied, "and if a storm catches us up here, we'd be in it for sure."

They were picking their way through the darkness when David's horse suddenly caught its leg between two rocks. The animal snorted with pain and jerked wildly about. The missionary was thrown to the ground but managed to keep from sliding into the gorge.

"I'm all right," he called to his anxious friend, "but it was close!"

THE HERMIT PRIEST

David Brainerd met many strange Indians in his travels, but none more strange than the hermit priest whom he met deep in the woods. When David first saw him, he was clad in an unusual assortment of skins, shells, and leaves.

"I am trying to restore the ancient religion to my people," he told the white man, "but they will not listen. They are happy with their woodland gods."

"I have something far better than either the ancient religion or the woodland gods," David assured the mournful Indian. "It is the Gospel of Jesus."

The priest listened carefully as the missionary told him the Christian story. It was a strange pair they made—David Brainerd, the frail white man, and the hideously dressed Indian priest. But they liked each other and

listened carefully to each other's words. After a while, the priest spoke to David.

"I think you know the God for whom I have been searching these many, many years. I will take Him as my Heavenly Father too."

"And you will want to tell your people of Him too," reminded the missionary, "for you want them to be as happy with the Christian faith as you are."

THE GIRL WHO LAUGHED

One day as the missionary was resting in his lodgings, he heard a timid knock on the door. Opening it, he saw a young Indian woman standing there.

"I have come to learn more about the religion you have been spreading among the people," she said. "I have heard that you do not believe in the many gods we and our fathers worship."

"I believe in the one God of the Bible," David assured her.

The woman laughed heartily as she spoke again. "You have a funny religion. It has only one God, while we have hundreds of gods. I think our gods are mightier than your single God."

She continued laughing, but just the same, she went to the place where David was preparing to preach. She listened carefully as he told everyone of God's salvation in Jesus. Her face became more serious as his words sank into her mind. She finally began to sob.

"Guttummaukalummeh! Guttummaukalummeh! Have mercy on me! Have mercy on me!"

The wonderful news soon spread through the woods that the laughing woman had been converted.

A NEW RELIGION

As the fame of the young missionary spread throughout the forests, the number of listeners grew. Many of them came out of curiosity, wanting to hear of this new religion that so many of their tribesmen had adopted.

"Have you seen Manntama since he has believed in the Christian religion?" one warrior would say to another. "He is as happy as a forest brook. He sings all day long about his new God."

"Yes, I have seen him. No longer does he quarrel with his brothers. He is too cheerful to fight with anyone. It must be a good religion that can make a friendly warrior out of Manntama!"

So whenever the Indians heard that the white preacher with the "Book of God" was arriving, they set aside their weapons and tools to hear him. As many as one hundred Indians often sat in the clearing among their wigwams and turned attentive ears to the preacher's words. Many of them bowed their heads where they sat and asked for God's mercy.

"Now we will be as happy as the others," the newly converted Indians would say, "for we have Jesus in our hearts too."

THE MAN WITH THE BOOK

The missionary was a great curiosity to the Indian children. Many of them had never seen a white man before. So when they heard their fathers speaking of the mysterious man who invaded the woods with only a big book, they wondered at his courage.

"Even the bravest warriors do not go into the forests without a strong bow and a quiver full of arrows," they remarked.

"What is in the big, black book under his arm? Is it some new kind of rifle that can scare away the wolves and wildcats?"

"I will run and tell the warriors that he is coming!"

David soon overcame the children's fears by telling them the simple Gospel story. Their eyes grew wide as they heard of the wonderful life of Jesus.

"Now we know why you are so brave," the children finally said. "God Himself goes with you into the woods. Please tell us more about Him."

David established several schools where the children were trained. No more would they spend their days just playing in the woods. Now they learned how to farm and sew and build. Best of all, they heard more of the Gospel!

WAR DANCE

One of the most exciting ceremonies David witnessed as he traveled among the

people was a war dance performed at the village of a tribe of Delaware Indians. He had journeyed to the village to preach the Gospel but found the tribesmen busily preparing for a ceremonial dance.

In the center of a great clearing, a huge fire was beginning to throw brilliant arrows of flame into the surrounding darkness. Around the fire were gathered the young braves and older priests. As the flames leaped up, so did the Indians. Screeching horribly, they pranced in a wide circle around the fire.

"Eeeeeeaaaaahhhhh!"

"Waaaaaaaeeeeeeeeeee!"

All night long they kept up the mad parade. David wanted desperately to tell them of the Gospel but decided that it was best not to interfere at this time. Standing quietly in the shadows, he watched the noisy ceremony for several hours. Toward morning the weary Indians slipped off to their wigwams.

The next day they heard the Gospel story from the white missionary.

David realized that many Indians who would not come to hear a white man preach would surely be curious enough to hear the preaching of a fellow tribesman. So he gathered about him several stout Christian warriors and spoke to them.

"I want each of you to be a missionary to your own people. Go and tell them the Gospel just as I have told it to you."

"But we are not preachers," they protested. "We can't even read the Bible. How can we expect anyone to believe us?"

"Do you think you could do it if I went with you?"

"Yes."

"Could you do it if God went with you?"

"Yes, we could."

"Then God will go with you and give you strength, just as He gave me strength."

"You are right," the Indians admitted. "We will go."

"All God asks is that you do your best with what He has given you. Now, go."

David's heart leaped happily as he saw the Christian warriors return to the camps of their own peoples.

DAVID GOES HOME

From the very beginning, David Brainerd knew that the damp forests were not good for him. But the preaching of the Gospel was far more important to him than his own health.

"Maybe you should forget about going back into the forests," friends told him as he came home for a rest. "Maybe, if you take it easy for a few months, you can return to the Indians."

"The minute I am able to get to my feet, I will head for the camping grounds," he cheerfully replied. "I may not have much longer to preach."

And it was God's plan that the faithful David Brainerd should not preach much longer. His work was like that of a man sowing seeds in fertile ground, making it ready for others to reap a rich harvest.

Though David went home to God while still a young man, his life is an inspiration to others to this very day. What he accomplished among the New England Indians may also be achieved among the peoples of Asia or Africa or South America. Young David Brainerd proved that God's man can succeed in spite of hardships and handicaps.

JOHN G. PATON

MISSIONARY TO THE SOUTH SEAS

Story by Vernon Howard

"... A MISSIONARY!"

One evening a young teacher in Scotland hurried home where he found a close friend waiting for him.

"Joseph," the teacher spoke to his friend, "I've made up my mind."

"About what?" the friend asked.

"I'm going to become a missionary!"

"A missionary?" Joseph looked at the teacher in surprise. "You are already a Bible teacher and Sunday school worker. But a missionary! Why?"

"Because," the young teacher went on, "the Lord has called me."

Joseph was silent for a moment. Then he suddenly straightened in his chair. "Then you'll have to take me with you," he exclaimed. "Where are we going?"

"To the New Hebrides."

Where are the New Hebrides? They are a group of lonely islands in the South Seas. And who was the young teacher? His name was John G. Paton.

John Paton was brought up by Godly parents in the Scottish highlands. As a young man, he took a lively part in church and Sunday school work. But he is not remembered today for the country of his birth. His name is famous when linked to certain cannibal islands.

Remember, then, *John G. Paton* and the *South Seas*.

CANNIBALS!

John immediately began preparing himself for a lifetime among the natives of the South Seas. He knew he must not only be able to preach the Gospel but must be handy with tools and medicines. He should know how to build a house, how to grow bountiful crops, and how to care for the sick.

His ship docked at Melbourne, Australia, where he had to find another vessel that would take him closer to the New Hebrides. The captain of an American ship agreed to take him and his party. When they finally arrived in the South Seas, they were met by a small missionary schooner, the *John Knox*. When the little craft was loaded with the missionary equipment, it was so heavy that it began to drift helplessly toward the nearby isle of Tanna.

"Tanna is a cannibal island," Paton was told. "It is the end of all of us if our schooner drifts ashore."

But prayer and hard work pulled the *John Knox* away from Tanna's dangerous coast. A short time later, the party landed at the tiny village of Aneityum, the mission headquarters.

Paton gazed about at the natives who crowded around the dock. So these were the people with whom he was going to live for the rest of his life! Well, they were not very pretty, but he was certain he was going to like them.

"NUNGSI NARI ENU?"

Tanna! John's first missionary adventures were to be among the cannibal tribes of this island. The fearful shores they had so desperately avoided in their drifting ship were now the object of his first bold thrust!

When he first landed on Tanna's soil, he found the painted tribesmen to be strangely gentle. Perhaps they were more curious than angry at the white invader. John took advantage of their temporary show of

friendliness. Settling himself in a hut among the breadfruit trees, he began to study the Tannese people. Stalking boldly among them, he picked up bits of their language.

"*Nungsi nari enu?*" he asked, holding up a branch. "What is this?"

When they told him how to say "branch" in Tannese, he strolled about, holding up other objects.

"*Nungsi nari enu?*"

"That is a sword."

"*Nungsi nari enu?*"

"We call that a cooking vessel."

He rapidly became acquainted with the Tannese people and their customs. This was the first and very important step. But he wondered how long he could count on the friendship of the islanders—after all, they were fierce cannibals who resented outside interference.

"*I AM NOT HURT!*"

Nahak!

This was a terrifying word to the South Sea islanders, for it meant witchcraft, or sorcery.

As with most pioneer missionaries, John Paton discovered that superstition had a fearful hold on the native mind.

"I stand before you," he declared one day, "to see just how powerful your *nahak* is. Go ahead. Try to harm me with your evil spells."

The angry priests sprang into action. Striking fire to a bundle of twigs, they began to chant and sway before it. Whirling about, they wildly threw their arms toward Paton, as if to strike him down with an invisible force.

"What is the matter?" the missionary shouted above their shrieks. "I am not the least bit harmed by your *nahak*."

For the rest of the afternoon, the baffled witch doctors danced crazily about, trying to arouse their false gods.

"*Nahak* can never hurt me," John reminded them, "for *nahak* is only a superstition."

When the exhausted priests finally admitted that their rites were useless, Paton again called out to them, this time in a kindly voice. "Come over here and sit before me. I will tell you of the powerful God of Heaven and Earth Who loves you."

"I AM STILL YOUR CHIEF!"

Paton knew that it would be easier to win the natives to the Gospel if he first won their leaders. One of his first converts was a young chief named Kowia. But, sadly, Kowia's own people turned against him when they heard he had become a Christian. They gathered outside the mission house where he lived.

"If you do not return to us and to our gods, we will no longer call you our chief," they threatened.

"I will not worship idols again," Kowia boldly declared, "for I am a child of the true God."

"Then we will take all your lands and breadfruit trees."

"Take everything I own on Tanna," he replied, "but I have everlasting life which you cannot take."

The warriors swarmed into the mission yard, waving their clubs over Kowia's head. The chief snatched one of them and whirled it at the ear of his nearest tormentor.

"Just because I am a Christian, it does not mean that I am a coward. Come closer and this club will let you know that I am still your chief!"

Seeing the fire in Kowia's eyes, the attackers fled. From that day forward, the chief was greeted with great respect as he went about his villages. Now, he was not only their chief—he was their teacher!

ATTACK!

Early one morning the missionary heard the warning peal of a conch shell horn. Peering outside, he saw the hills swarming with frenzied natives. No sooner had he rushed from his hut than the horde of howling cannibals broke loose.

It was a race for life. Scrambling recklessly down the nearest path, he reached a friendly settlement.

"The hill tribes are on the warpath," he warned the terrified villagers. "Hurry, cut down trees to block the trail!"

But the maddened warriors flooded after them, brushing aside the hasty barriers. Paton quickly summoned a few hardy natives and set out again, hoping somehow to dodge the pursuing cannibals. He finally reached the beach where they launched a canoe. They found themselves whirled about by frantic waves. The paddlers turned frightened eyes toward Paton.

"Better to be captured by cannibals than spilled into the jaws of sharks!" they cried.

The missionary directed them to make for a sheltered part of the beach. As soon as they were safe on dry ground again, he led them to the distant home of another missionary.

But the adventure was not over yet; in fact, it was just beginning!

A MIRACLE IN THE NIGHT

A short time later, while John was sleeping, he felt his dog tugging at his clothes. Knowing that the faithful animal was trying to warn him, he sprang to his feet. He found the hut surrounded by the pursuing cannibals who were setting fire to the mission building. Seizing a revolver in one hand and a tomahawk in the other, he dashed outside.

"Stop!" he shouted, but the word was scarcely out before shadowy figures grabbed him. Springing aside, he leveled his revolver.

"Keep away," he warned. "You shall be punished for burning the chapel. It is God's property, and He will protect it. And you cannot harm a hair of my head while God stands between us."

The warriors muttered angrily, each urging another to strike the first blow. Just as they were about to raise their clubs, a roaring sound filled the air. As if struck by an invisible hand, the attackers fell back. A few moments later, a terrific tornado of wind and rain struck.

"It is God's rain!" the frightened cannibals admitted as they saw the torrent miraculously quench the fire. Lowering their clubs, they darted into the storming darkness.

John Paton humbly thanked God for the miracle which had saved both his life and the chapel.

EXCITING TALES

Missionary John Paton decided that the time had now come for him to tell the outside world of his adventures. For how could Christian folks the world over pray for and support his work unless they knew of it? What a greater blessing would be upon his efforts with thousands of interested folks backing him up!

Taking with him a boxful of native idols, weapons, and other curious exhibits, he set sail from the South Seas. Visiting the churches of Australia, Scotland, and England, he told of his thrilling experiences among the island cannibals. The churches were crowded with Christians who listened with amazement and stared with fascination at the native objects.

"The most wonderful thing of all," he was told, wherever he went, "is that you escaped to tell us of your adventures!"

Now that his Gospel work was known, Paton determined to return to the islands and take up where he had left off. This time he headed for Aniwa, one of the smaller islands of the New Hebrides. Little Aniwa was only seven miles long and two miles wide and was surrounded by a belt of coral reef.

For the next fifteen years, the hardy Scotsman was to live on this tiny dot of land in the middle of the ocean!

THE TALKING CHIP!

With the help of friendly natives, Paton set about building a mission headquarters. During this work, a humorous incident occurred. The missionary found himself in need of some tools, so he scribbled a note on a chip of wood and handed it to one of the chiefs.

"Take this chip to Mrs. Paton. She will give you the tools I need."

The chief frowned. "How can this chip tell her what you want? Has it a tongue?"

"Take it to her at once," John requested. "She will understand, even if you do not."

"Whoever heard of wood speaking?" the baffled chief muttered as he shuffled away. When he handed the chip to Mrs. Paton, she quickly glanced at it and found the wanted tools. The amazed chief hurried back.

"This is wonderful!" he exclaimed. "The white teacher can make chips of wood speak for him!"

Paton patiently explained that Mrs. Paton had simply read the words he had written on the chip. He then went on to point out that the Bible could be read in much the same way.

It was one of the most startling miracles the islanders had seen at the hands of the white teacher. How clever were these people from the other side of the world. Why, they could print a whole book with thousands of tiny tongues in it!

LITTLE PRINCESSES

Not long after the mission house was completed, Chief Namakei appeared at the door. A little girl stood at his side.

"This is my daughter, Litsi Sore," said the chief. "I want to leave her with you."

"Why do you want her to live with us?" he was asked.

"Because I want her to grow up in a home where she can read the Bible and sing Christian songs. If she stays here, she will grow up to be a fine young lady."

Paton took the girl into his home, and Chief Namakei went gratefully home.

A short time later, a second chief came to the mission. At his side stood another little girl.

"Please take my daughter into your house too," he pleaded. "I want her to learn of Christian things."

Paton recognized the man as the brother of Chief Namakei. He told him that he, too, could leave his daughter.

The two bright-eyed little princesses were as busy as monkeys about the mission home. They ran errands and helped Mrs. Paton with the housework. On Sundays they helped the other island children with their Bible lessons.

"Please take us to the mission house next Sunday," children from all over Aniwa pleaded with their parents.

THE MIRACULOUS WELL

As beautiful an island as Aniwa was, it did not have enough fresh water to suit John Paton. Taking up a pick and shovel, he made an announcement:

"I am going to dig a well to see if we can strike fresh water. I want you to help me."

The Aniwans looked at him with baffled faces. What miracle was the missionary going to perform now? How could water be found beneath the ground? Impossible!

"Rain comes from the sky down to the earth," they solemnly told him. "How can you find it by digging a deep hole?"

Paton swung his pick into the earth. "In my country across the sea, we have many wells that give up sweet water. I think we may find it here too."

But the natives refused to help, believing it to be a useless task. Yet, they could not keep from crowding around, peering curiously into the dark hole where the missionary worked alone. As he went deeper, a few of the men finally agreed to haul away the elevated buckets of raw earth.

"Water! Fresh water!" The cry suddenly rang out as a bucket arose, its sides spilling over with the cool liquid. The jubilant islanders swarmed to the well.

"God has given us this water," Paton told them. "We must use it for the good of everyone."

END OF THE IDOLS

After the wonderful well was completed, Chief Namakei came to Paton with a request.

"I believe this well is a sign of God's love for us. May I preach to my people next Sunday?"

Paton gave his consent, so the chief appeared before a great crowd of islanders the following Sunday. Swinging his tomahawk wildly, he began to preach.

"People of Aniwa, we have seen a great miracle at the hands of the Christian teacher. It is wonderful to know there is a God who can bring water from the depths of the ground. Our idols could not perform any of the miracles we have seen since the white teacher came to us. From this day, I am a follower of God and His Son. We must all become followers of this true God."

Still twirling his tomahawk, the fiery chief gave a final command.

"Let us bring all our idols of wood and stone and cast them at the feet of the Christian missionary. We will burn and bury them—destroy them forever!"

All week long, the happy islanders marched into the mission yard with their loads of idols. The roaring flames quickly consumed the strange figures.

A new way of life had come to the tiny island of Aniwa!

THE CHIEF GOES TO SCHOOL!

Chief Namakei had now become a leader among his people in the Gospel work. But he was eager to know more of this new and joyous Christian religion. He soon had the opportunity, for John Paton was now able to print brief portions of the Bible on an old printing press.

"Please give me one of your talking books," pleaded the chief, "so I can hear it speak of Jesus."

When the missionary gave him a few pages, the chief happily put them before his eyes. His face clouded with disappointment an instant later.

"But it does not speak to me," he complained. "I cannot hear it."

"You must first learn to read," John told him. "Here, I will fit you with a pair of spectacles."

With great wonderment, the chief saw the letters grow clearer as he gazed through the glasses.

"Now, I will teach you the alphabet," Paton continued. "We will take three letters at a time."

Taking a stick, the missionary traced the letters *A, B,* and *C* in the dust. "You must fix these letters in your mind," Chief Namakei was told. "As soon as you learn the whole alphabet, the Bible will speak to you."

From that day, Chief Namakei became a teacher of the Bible to his own people.

PATON VISITS WITH THE PRESIDENT

Paton knew that the wonders of the missionary work on the little isle of Aniwa could be repeated on other South Sea islands. But he also knew it would take many more missionaries. In order again to attract attention to the South Seas, he wrote the story of his adventures among the island cannibals. To his astonishment, the book made him famous. Once more he decided to make a tour of the world, which included a cross-country journey of the United States.

Wherever he stopped, he found eager crowds waiting to hear from his own lips the stories they had first read in his book. While in Washington, D.C., he was invited to lunch at the White House by

President Grover Cleveland. The President was a Godly man who listened carefully to Paton's exciting stories.

"It would help a great deal if the government of the United States would stop American ships from selling guns to the islanders or from taking them as slaves," Paton told the President. "I hope you will do everything you can to stop these evil practices."

President Cleveland expressed a deep interest in Paton's work. He also promised the missionary that he would do everything he could for the peoples of the South Seas.

"I WILL COME AGAIN."

Wherever he went among Christians of the outside world, John Paton told of the need for new missionaries. To show this need, he often told of an adventure off the island of Ambrim. His ship was floating offshore when two natives paddled alongside.

"You missionary?" they called up.

"Yes, I am a missionary," Paton replied.

"You not have guns? You come to tell us of peaceful things?"

"I have come to help you," they were assured.

Satisfied that the missionary meant them no harm, they invited him ashore. He was instantly confronted by a painted native who grabbed Paton's arm and began to chatter noisily.

"You good white teacher. You stay!"

"I cannot come again for another year," the warrior was told. "We have many other islands to visit."

"No!" the warrior cried in despair. "We want missionary *now!*"

But Paton had to cast off, leaving only the promise that a missionary would come to them later.

The young teacher who had come from Scotland so many years before had finished his work. Like little flickering candlelights, the Gospel gleamed in the dark islands of the lonely South Pacific. Hundreds of islanders were now leading Christian lives because of the stalwart man who was both their teacher and their friend—John G. Paton.

ANN JUDSON
FRIEND OF BURMA

Story by Vernon Howard

"Ann! Ann Hasseltine! There you go dreaming again. What is it this time?"

The girl with the flaming cheeks and the curly hair laughed as she turned to her friends.

"Oh, I was just thinking of how wonderful it would be to sail to faraway lands."

"Well, you are not a sailor, young Miss Hasseltine. You are just a little Massachusetts girl like the rest of us, and you will probably spend your life sewing and baking on a quiet New England farm."

As Ann sat on the mossy bank overlooking the Merrimac River, she wondered if her friends were right. Most of her companions in the little village of Bradford *would* spend their lives in the quietness of the country. It was, she admitted, a happy and peaceful life. And there was always plenty of excitement to be found in church and school and social activities.

"Besides, Ann," one of her friends remarked, "who would look after you if you suddenly shipped to the other side of the world? You couldn't go alone."

Pretty Ann Hasseltine smiled. "Yes, I suppose I would need someone at my side."

ANN ASKS QUESTIONS

It was an exciting time for Bradford when a group of young ministers arrived one day with a bold proposal.

"We would like to go as missionaries to foreign shores. We need your prayers and assistance."

Ann thrilled at the thought of these young men carrying the Gospel to the four corners of the globe. Never before had an American gone to a foreign land as a missionary!

Later she asked her father, "Do you suppose that I could ever be a missionary?"

Mr. Hasseltine smiled fondly at his youngest daughter. "Maybe you haven't heard some of the terrible stories our sailors tell about Africa and Asia. It would be hard enough for a man to go—but for a slip of a girl like you? No, Ann, I think not."

"But the heathen women need the Gospel as well as the men," Ann replied, "and I think an American girl like myself could do it as well as anyone."

"You will have your chance to hear more about it tomorrow," said Ann's father. "You see, several of these young ministers are coming here for dinner."

"THEY ARE COMING!"

Early the next morning, Ann and her mother busied themselves about the kitchen. The dinner they were to serve was to be a very special one, for the guests themselves were very special. Before long the kitchen table was loaded with delicious pies, cakes, and breads.

"Look, Mother," Ann suddenly called from the window. "They are coming!"

"You should put on a fresh dress, Ann," her mother advised. "I want you to help serve our guests."

Ann's heart thumped excitedly as the ministers entered the house. One by one she made their acquaintance. One of them was a brown-eyed, pleasant-faced young man named Adoniram Judson. Ann turned shyly away as Adoniram smiled at her.

Ann listened attentively as she passed around the table with her steaming dishes.

"We must make this effort *now*," the positive voice of Adoniram Judson rose above the conversation. "Millions of heathen in scores of foreign lands are without even a single Gospel messenger. It is our Christian duty to go to them at once."

ADONIRAM VISITS ANN

Adoniram Judson called many more times at the Hasseltine home. He often talked with Mr. Hasseltine about the proposed missionary adventure. But more often he talked with the youngest Hasseltine girl. One day he asked her a question.

"Ann, you know that I intend to take the Gospel across the sea. Will you go with me as my helper and my wife?"

Ann was thrilled at the thought of joining this splendid young man in a lifetime of missionary work. But she knew there were obstacles in the way.

"I do want to be with you wherever you go," she told Adoniram, "but I want to be sure that I will be a help and not a hindrance. So many of my friends think it is a wild idea for a woman to be a missionary. I used to think it would be a romantic adventure—but now I am not so sure."

"We would miss the comfort of our New England homes," Adoniram admitted, "but we can't think of ourselves when so many are without the Gospel."

Ann thought and prayed for several weeks. Then one day, when Adoniram called, she took him to one side.

"I *know* what I should do. We will go together to wherever the Gospel is needed."

TO FOREIGN SHORES

Things happened swiftly for Adoniram and Ann Judson once they touched the soil of India. As soon as they arrived, they were told they must leave.

"You cannot stay in India," they were told. "You must return to America on the very ship that brought you here."

The young American missionaries refused. Instead, they decided to go for a temporary stay at the island of Mauritius, which was four thousand miles away. Once they established themselves there, they could again make plans for return to an Asiatic country.

The voyage to Mauritius was stormy and dangerous, but they finally arrived safely. Immediately they set up a headquarters for the Gospel work.

"We are going back to India," Adoniram announced in a surprisingly brief time. "If that's where God wants us, that's where we'll stay."

But once more they were refused admission to the country. Ann now began to believe that God wanted them somewhere else.

"Adoniram," she said to her husband, "I think we should go to Burma."

They had to make an immediate decision. It was either Burma or America. To return home would mean defeat. To sail to Burma might mean incredible hardship, even death.

"If I were alone, I would not hesitate to go to Burma at once," said Adoniram to Ann. "But I don't want to ask you to share the dangers with me."

"It is settled," Ann replied with determination. "We are both going to Burma. If God wants us there, He will provide for us."

When they arrived in Rangoon, the capital of Burma, they found it as miserable as they had expected. It was a primitive city with dirt and decay everywhere. The natives lived in shabby bamboo huts that faced muddy roads.

As Ann passed through the city, she was surrounded by curious Burmese. They had seen Englishmen before, but a white woman—and an *American*—was a strange sight indeed. Some of the bolder natives even pulled at her clothing and touched her soft, wavy hair.

Ann delighted the Burmese women by smiling confidently back at them.

ANN AT COURT

Ann and her husband established themselves in the mission home of Felix Carey, the only other Christian missionary in all Burma. Within a few days they had settled themselves and were ready to begin their work.

"The first thing we must do is learn as much as we can about the Burmese language," Adoniram told Ann. "After we learn to speak the language, I want to translate the Bible into Burmese. Won't it be wonderful when the people can read the Gospel in their own language?"

When Ann was not helping her husband, she applied herself to learning more of the land of Burma and its people. Like Adoniram, she realized the importance of understanding the men and women with whom she would live for the rest of her life.

One of her interesting first experiences was her introduction to the wife of the viceroy. The viceroy was the supreme ruler of the Burmese people. When Ann was brought to court, the viceroy's wife received her politely and asked her many questions about America.

"PLEASE TELL US MORE"

Before long, Ann had gathered a group of thirty women and children about her. Eagerly they listened as the American missionary told them of God's grace. As the Gospel truth gradually unfolded to them, they began to ask all sorts of questions.

"We want to worship your God, but we cannot see Him," one woman stated.

"Yes," another went on, "we have our idols of wood and stone. We can bow before them because we can see them. But how can we bow before an invisible God?"

Ann wisely understood how strange the Gospel must be to people who were raised in superstition and idol worship. She patiently answered all their questions. After a while, they began to ask questions that showed how much they had learned.

"Please, Miss Ann, tell us again how God came to Earth to save us from our sins. Did

He come to save the peoples of all countries?"

"How soon will we be able to read the Bible in our own language? We can hardly wait."

A ROYAL CARRIAGE!

The months passed swiftly as the Judsons kept themselves busy from early morning to late at night. Ann divided her time between helping her husband and running the home and entertaining its many visitors.

Every once in a while a royal elephant would ponderously amble up to the mission house, and one of the viceroy's servants would call out:

"Her majesty wishes you to come to the palace for the afternoon. Please bring your religious books."

Ann was delighted to accept the royal summons. She hoped and prayed that the viceroy's wife might become a Christian. What a testimony it would be to all Burma if the queen would publicly announce herself as a Christian! One day when Ann presented herself before the queen, the royal lady announced:

"I am pleased with the Christian religion. I have permitted one of my daughters to study it for a while. I think that Christians such as you and your husband are good for our nation. Yes, it might be a good thing if all the Burmese people were Christians."

STORIES OF BURMA

One evening, after Ann had had a long, weary day, her husband sat by her side and spoke.

"Ann, you are very tired. I think you need to return to America for a rest."

Ann objected to leaving Adoniram but finally agreed that it was the only thing to do. "Besides," her husband told her, "you can help our work enormously just by telling the folk of New England about it. Think of all the Christians who will begin praying for the Burmese people if you just tell them of the need."

When Ann arrived in her beloved New England, she found her husband's words to be true. Men and women all over the country were fascinated by her tales of missionary adventure in Burma. Wherever she went, she found eager audiences ready to pray for Burma. They even persuaded Ann to write a book of her experiences.

After taking time out for a rest, she made plans for her return to Burma. Adoniram had been lonely for a long time now, and she was lonely for him too.

WAR!

Ann was met at Rangoon by her husband. By boat they pushed their way toward the city of Ava. "I have established myself at Ava so I can see the king more often," Adoniram explained. "I hope he will give us more liberty to preach the Gospel."

As they neared their destination, they were amazed to see an immense fleet of Burmese vessels bearing down on them. Before long, they were surrounded by the boats, which were loaded with angry-looking soldiers.

"Who are you and where are you going?" the challenge rang across the water to them.

When Adoniram replied that they were American missionaries on their way to Ava, they were permitted to pass. But Adoniram shook his head dismally.

"I am afraid that war will come between Burma and England," he said. "And when it does, all white men in the country will be branded as traitors."

One morning as the Judsons were preparing their meal, a troop of Burmese soldiers stormed into the house and took Adoniram prisoner.

"We are at war," a soldier announced. "The American spy must go to prison."

COURAGEOUS ANN

Though Ann was stunned by her husband's arrest, she made immediate visits to the royal palace and stated her case before the government officials. She even saw the queen herself, but the answer was always the same.

"The white man is a prisoner and will remain a prisoner as long as the war lasts."

Ann followed whenever Adoniram was moved from prison to prison. Whenever she

could persuade a jailor to let her see her husband, she brought him food and medicine. But these visits were rarely for more than a few minutes.

Ann's courage and faith brought tears of joy to the weary Adoniram and made his chains more bearable.

"God has a plan for us in all this," he assured her. "We know that He permits only those things which are good for us."

The frantic efforts to free her husband began to wear away Ann's strength. For weeks at a time, she lay helpless in her hut, attended only by her native friends. It became impossible for her to gather enough strength to visit Adoniram.

"I FORGIVE YOU"

One day, as Ann lay weakly on her bed, she heard footsteps approaching. Raising her head, she saw the figure of a man enter the room. Her heart leaped with joy as she saw that it was Adoniram. They tearfully greeted each other and gave thanks to God who had spared their lives.

"The war is over," Adoniram told Ann. "All white men are free."

With immense relief the two missionaries began a downstream journey that brought them under the protection of the British flag. The general in charge of the camp staged a huge dinner to celebrate the occasion. While a band played a lively march, the Judsons entered the banquet hall. It was here that Ann displayed the gentle Christian spirit that was hers. In front of her stood one of the Burmese officials who had mocked her when she had pleaded for his help some months ago. A word from Ann and he might be tossed into the very prison where Adoniram had suffered.

"You have nothing to fear," Ann told the frightened man. "I forgive you for everything."

BUSY DAYS

It was now thirteen years since the brave Ann had sailed with her husband to the hostile country of Burma. Together they had suffered much for the Gospel's sake. But their most important work was yet to come.

"My work in translating the Bible into Burmese is nearly done," Adoniram joyfully exclaimed. "Think of the tens of thousands of people who will soon be able to read the story of the Cross for themselves. It has taken a lot of hard work, but I would do it a thousand times again."

A small printing press gave them the opportunity of publishing tracts and booklets. These silent Gospel messengers were scattered far and wide over the country.

Knowing how important it was to her husband to have as much time as possible, Ann did everything she could to free him from extra duties. She helped with his writings, taught classes, and received visitors who came to inquire about the Gospel.

Adoniram was grateful for such a splendid wife who shared his ministry so courageously. He knew that without her he could not have succeeded so well.

A NEW WORK

After Adoniram's release from prison, the Judsons established a new work at the village of Amhurst. But shortly after their arrival, Adoniram was called by the British government to assist them in drawing up a peace treaty with Burma. At first he refused to leave Ann, but she persuaded him.

"I had to leave you once when it seemed the best thing to do. Now I think it best that you go. I can carry on here."

While her husband was away, Ann supervised the erection of new buildings. It was long and difficult work for the frail American heroine. In spite of her weariness, she wrote an encouraging letter to her husband:

"After all our sufferings and afflictions, I cannot but hope that God has mercy and a blessing in store for us. Let us strive to obtain it by our prayers and holy life."

Ann grew weaker as the days slipped by. Finally, after one last tender letter to Adoniram, she went home to the Lord.

The brave Ann Hasseltine of New England had now become a friend of an entire nation. She will always be known as Ann Judson—friend of Burma.

PANDITA RAMABAI
HEROINE OF INDIA

Story by Vernon Howard

"HURRY, RAMABAI."

"Pick up your things, Ramabai; we are going."

The little girl of India looked sadly at her older brother. "Why do we wander so much? I wish we could settle down in this nice village."

Her brother shook his head. "You know why, Ramabai. Father and Mother must take us wherever there is food. It is worth trudging the road all day if we can find a cupful of rice at its end."

"But we never find more than just a taste. Sometimes Mother and Father almost faint from hunger."

"India is a poor country," her brother reminded, as he helped Ramabai with her load.

A few moments later, Ramabai and her family were slowly making their way down the dusty road. The little Hindu girl did not understand why it was so hard to live. She was too young to realize that in India millions were hungry much of the time. The fields did not produce nearly enough to support the great multitudes who lived there.

But as young as she was, Ramabai began to ponder. "Couldn't something be done for India's hungry and homeless people?"

Maybe, when she was a bit taller, she could do something. But until then, she could only wander.

READING THE PURANAS

When the years of hardship took away her family, Ramabai and her brother found themselves alone in a frightening world. The orphans had no place to turn but to the unfriendly roads.

"Maybe I can find work in Calcutta," her brother suggested. So they set out for that great city. But food and work were as scarce there as anywhere else. Back and forth across the country the brother and sister wandered, finding a mouthful of rice here or a cluster of berries there. Often they slept under the stars, cold and weary. One night the air was so freezing they went to a riverbank and buried themselves in dry sand.

"Maybe we can earn money for food if I read the *Puranas* in public," Ramabai proposed. The *Puranas* are the sacred Hindu writings.

Standing on the steps of the temples or sitting by the roadside, Ramabai read to the passersby. Sometimes a grateful listener would press a small coin or a few grains of rice into her small, brown hand.

But the more she read the sacred writings of the Brahman religion, the more she doubted them.

"What a weak religion is this that shows so little pity for the poor. Isn't there some other religion that shows more love for the suffering?"

PANDITA RAMABAI!

As Ramabai grew to be a young woman, she was shocked to see that home life for multitudes of Indian women was nothing more than slavery. She determined to help her countrywomen gain their rightful position of honor in Indian life.

"We will go again from city to village to tell all India that its women must be given a new respect," she told her brother.

"But—" he hesitated, "no one has ever done this before. They will think it very strange. India sleeps while the women suffer."

"Then we will wake them up!"

Back to Calcutta, the city where they had almost starved a few years before, came Ramabai and her brother. The brave and dignified Hindu girl immediately astonished the Pandits—the wise scholars—with her high intelligence.

"Why do you wish to change the established customs of our country?" they asked when they had called her before them.

"What good will it do to educate our women?"

"And how do you, a mere girl of twenty-two years, expect to overthrow the customs we have had for centuries?"

The Pandits were so impressed with Ramabai's forthright replies that they gave her the title of *Pandita*, which made her the only woman in all India with that honor!

ENGLAND—AND AN EDUCATION

Pandita Ramabai traveled widely, telling India of its sad neglect of its women and children. During one of these journeys, she met a kind lawyer who later became her husband. But her happy marriage was cut short by her husband's sudden death. Once more the brave Indian girl found herself alone, except that now she had a bundle of comfort in her little daughter Manorama.

About this time Ramabai began to feel the need for a broader education. She wisely reasoned that proper training would mold her into a more forceful worker among her people. She decided to take Manorama and go to England where she could study under the great teachers of that country.

Ramabai's doubts of the Hindu religion had increased as she grew older. Even as a child, she knew the gods of stone and brass were not for her. One day in Calcutta, she had been given portions of the Bible which she eagerly searched. Her spirit stirred joyfully as she read the Gospel. At last she was beginning to see light in a dark world.

So education was not the only thing she found in England. Not long after her arrival, she found the Saviour!

She gave her life fully to God. "Now, there will be two of us working together," she happily exclaimed, "the Saviour—and I!"

AMERICA—AND A THRILL

Ramabai's days in England were busily spent in studying the English language, science, mathematics, and literature. "I am going to visit America before returning to my country," she told her friends, when her schooling was finally completed.

When she landed on the American shore, she intended staying only a week or two. Instead, she stayed three years.

America would not let her go. Pandita Ramabai, the humble Hindu girl, was a heroine! Americans wanted to hear this courageous Indian widow who had dedicated her life to the women of her native land. She was overwhelmed with invitations from church and community groups. Her lectures drew thousands of fascinated listeners.

"The many, many millions of my people serve fantastic gods," she told of her native land. "It may seem strange to you, but even the cows are held sacred and are allowed to roam the streets. . . .

"India's rulers are called Maharajahs; they live in magnificent temples; they have great armies which control the lives of the people. . . .

"The most remarkable social system among my people is the caste system. High-caste Hindus do not eat food prepared by low-caste or associate with them in any way."

"HOME OF WISDOM"

Ramabai returned to India with a firm resolution—her aim in life would be the rescue of India's widows and children and their salvation through faith in Christ. Though she was certain the work would be difficult, she was also certain that, by God's grace, she would succeed.

Her first task was the erection of a home in the city of Poona. "We will call it *Sharada Sadan*, the Home of Wisdom," she declared, "and we welcome the outcast and hungry to its door."

The next few weeks were cheerfully spent in preparing the house and grounds for the expected guests.

"We must plant gardens and orchards where we can grow our own vegetables and fruits," Ramabai pointed out, remembering her own girlhood years of hunger. "And we should obtain a dairy herd to supply us with milk and butter and cheese."

"We can teach the girls to weave and sew and design their own clothing," her assistant added. "Busy hands make happy hearts."

Ramabai's heart overflowed with joy one afternoon when her daughter came into her room at the newly finished Sharada Sadan. Manorama's dark eyes flashed happily as she spoke. "Mother, I want to help make the Sharada Sadan a Christian home. I have taken Jesus as my Saviour too."

QUESTIONS!

Exciting days followed the opening of the home. From farmlands and cities came homeless girls asking for shelter beneath its protecting roof. Entering the Sharada Sadan was like stepping from a dark valley to a sunny hilltop. And waiting to welcome the outcast Hindu girls was the sympathetic Pandita Ramabai.

"The Sharada Sadan is your home for as long as you need one," she greeted. "We must all work alongside each other and for each other. If you need help at any time, please come to me."

How the little Hindu girls loved her! She was their mother, their teacher, and friend. Like frisky, friendly puppies, they followed her about the Sharada Sadan. More than once Ramabai had to set aside her own work to listen patiently to the chatter of lively tongues.

"*Bai*," they addressed her, using the usual Hindu title for housemother, "today we were taught to use a strange thing called a microscope. What makes little things so big through a microscope?"

"*Bai*," another question popped up before she could answer the first, "if the world spins around like a ball, why do we not fall off?"

"*Bai*, why do you read the book of the Englishman's God? What is in the Bible?"

"COME TO US..."

"There are many captive girls who have never heard of our home here in Poona," said Ramabai. "Somehow I must see that they know of us."

"You must be very careful," she was advised. "You will be in danger if you go boldly into the cities. The Hindu priests are enemies of the Sharada Sadan. They say you are encouraging the slaves to rebel against their masters."

"And I intend to keep right on doing just that. I may even disguise myself in order to go in and out among the girls. I am going first to Brindaban, where there are hundreds of wretched slave girls."

Clothing herself in the garb of a poor pilgrim, Ramabai set out for the distant city. Unrecognized by the wicked priests, she quietly told the Hindu girls that she had come to their rescue.

"If you can escape from your masters, you will find refuge at the Sharada Sadan. You do

not have to remain here in slavery. Your masters have no right to hold you. Please come as soon as you can. We will watch for you."

Leaving this message of hope, Ramabai returned safely to her Christian fortress at Poona. Her expeditions were rewarded, for every once in a while, the door would open to admit a hopeful runaway.

A WELCOME SIGHT

Ramabai did not always find it necessary to disguise herself in order to do her best work. Often she boldly announced her intentions to tour the countryside, teaching Christianity and passing out food and clothing.

"As Christians, it is our duty to provide food and garments to the undernourished," she reminded her helpers before they started. "Be sure that you load the wagon with baskets of rice, lentils, butter, and coconuts."

The sight of her heavy cart, drawn by two splendid white bulls, was a welcome sight to the hungry Hindus. They crowded around, eager for both the gifts and the words of comfort she had for them.

"*Salaam, Bai! Salaam, Bai!*" they cried their thanks.

"It is by God's grace that I am able to give you these things," she reminded. "If you believe in His Son, you will also receive eternal life."

Sometimes timid little girls approached the wagon, their eyes dark and tearful.

"We have heard of the wonderful Sharada Sadan. Do you have room for us?"

Ramabai's heart ached when she heard the pitiful stories of these unhappy girls. She lovingly invited them to return with her.

"How I thank God," she often said, "that He has made this home possible."

ESCAPE!

The chief enemies of the Sharada Sadan were the Hindu priests. They resented their slaves being taken from them by the Christian Pandita. But Ramabai stood firm; the girls must be freed from their shackles.

One little maid from the village of Gujerathi was purposely sent to a hospital at Bombay, where it was hoped she would be lost from her enslavers. But the cunning priests tracked her down and demanded her return. One of Ramabai's friends called on the girl at her sickbed.

"Do you want to go back to Gujerathi?" the frail girl was asked.

Her eyes widened fearfully. "No, *Bai*," she pleaded. "Don't let them take me. They beat me with whips and make me sleep in the cold. Please, *Bai*, let me go to the home of the Christians."

The wicked priests watched the hospital day and night, hoping to catch the girl when she left. But the friendly hospital matron permitted the girl and her Christian friend to leave in secret. When the priests discovered her escape, they angrily demanded that the police bring her back. But the Christian police chief refused, leaving the girl from Gujerathi safe beneath Ramabai's roof.

MUKTI!

The fame of the Sharada Sadan had now reached all over the world. Christians were astonished and delighted with the brilliant work being done by the girl who had once been a wandering waif herself. Pandita Ramabai's name was spoken with admiration and respect.

But the home at Poona was only the beginning of her achievements. One afternoon, a helper came to her.

"Ramabai, our walls are just about to burst; we need more room. I think we should open another home."

"Where do you think we should build it?"

"At Khedgaon. There is splendid farmland there which can be developed into orchards and gardens."

"I know the place," Ramabai nodded. "It has a real need for a Christian home."

"Then we will go there?" the helper hopefully asked.

"At once!" Ramabai responded.

Like wildfire, enthusiasm for the new Sharada Sadan spread among Ramabai's girls. They had been helped by the home at Poona. Now they would help build one for the girls at Khedgaon!

"What can we do to help?" they asked.

"You can pray," they were told, "and when it is built, you can pray for the girls who come there."

The happy day arrived when the home was completed. "We will call it *Mukti*," said Ramabai, "for the word means 'salvation.'"

STRANGE INDIA

The visitor to India is always drawn to the magnificent temples and palaces which served the powerful emperors of the past. The Taj Mahal, near the city of Agra, and other mighty marble buildings are famous throughout the world. Though many centuries old, their dazzling splendor persists to this day.

Ramabai found it interesting to visit these historic places. While touring the ruined palace of an ancient Mogul emperor, she asked her guide a question.

"I understand the emperor was a cruel man who chained his slaves in dark dungeons beneath the palace. Is this right?"

The guide at first denied the existence of dungeons but finally admitted that the underground was combed with cells and torture chambers. Ramabai and her companion insisted that he take them below, so he opened a trapdoor and led the way.

In the light of the guide's torch, the two ladies saw the musty prisons where the slaves were chained. As unpleasant as it was, the two Christians went the full length of the dark dungeons.

"It is good that we saw this," Ramabai remarked as they climbed into the bright sunlight again. "It will keep us reminded that India's religions are as cruel as its dungeons. Oh, how badly our country needs the beautiful Gospel!"

RAMABAI'S GIRLS

Famine!

This is always a dreadful word in India. When the fields fail to produce even their meager crops, India faces disaster. Famine—the lack of food—is one of India's greatest enemies.

Ramabai once journeyed to a famine district where she found three hundred hungry girls. As her heart went out in aching sympathy, she began to wonder what could be done for them. The Mukti mission was already crowded; it would take an overwhelming flood of supplies to care for these famished and ill-clothed outcasts.

But the Pandita was as resourceful as she was sympathetic. Taking up her pen, she wrote the story of her efforts, telling of the need for help. The story was published in a Bombay newspaper which was under the direction of Christian editors.

"Picture, if you can," she wrote, "hundreds of young girls, wandering the streets, day and night, hungry and homeless and friendless. Many of them wander slowly, for they are weak and sickly. They have no hope, for their own false religion has failed them. They are spiritless and desperate."

Christian readers were shocked into action. Funds rolled into the Mukti treasury—and Ramabai went looking for her three hundred girls!

WORK TO DO!

The following years were lively ones for Ramabai. Mukti meant busy days and nights, teaching, traveling, building, and lecturing. She even found time to write songs and poetry for the native hymnals.

From humble beginnings, the two homes had now grown so large that almost eight hundred girls were being sheltered. Ramabai's staff of assistants had swelled to over a hundred.

"We must follow the practice we first established at Poona," Ramabai instructed her helpers. "Each girl should be taught a useful occupation, so that when she leaves the home, she can find employment."

"What kinds of work should they be taught?" she was asked.

"Whatever is most suitable for each. Some can become nurses; others can learn to weave; still others can be taught to tend the herds and gardens. Those who know their Bibles well enough can become teachers, while the older girls can take on the responsibilities of housekeeping. Whatever they learn, there will be a need for it."

So the work prospered. Whenever a girl was ready to leave the home to begin a new and happy life, there was always another needy one to take her place.

"Mukti is never so crowded that we cannot invite another poor girl beneath its roof," said Ramabai.

MUKTI—CHRISTIAN FORTRESS!

Many eventful years had passed since little Ramabai and her family first trudged the lonely Indian roads. Then, she was just another hungry Hindu child, not knowing whether she would grow up or whether she would perish. Her only gods were made of stone and brass and could not hear her pleas.

When she became a Christian, she found herself with a real purpose in life and a wonderful story to tell. Before long, the entire country was listening to the Pandita Ramabai, the courageous girl who had arisen above her miserable circumstances to become a famous figure.

Ramabai's success caused millions to wonder. How was it possible? How could a frail outcast become known all over the world? Surely, she was just a plain Hindu girl, much the same as millions of her sisters.

Could it be that her religion—her relationship with Christ—helped her?

"What God has done for me, He can also do for you," she told her wondering countrymen. "But you must destroy your false idols and worship God alone."

To the end of her days, Ramabai searched for the outcast girls who needed her. Typical of the girls she influenced was one child who slipped quietly up while Ramabai was taking the names of those who were to be baptized.

"Bai, Bai, mere, nam, likna!" the girl pleaded. "Please, Mother, write my name too!"

Pandita Ramabai gave food, shelter, clothing, and education to the desperately poor of her country; but more than that, she gave them the message of hope for this life and eternal joy in Heaven forever, through faith in Christ.

She told them that Jesus Christ, the Son of God, came to Earth and lived as a man; that He died upon the Cross to pay the penalty of sin, which is death; and that He rose again from the dead and now offers eternal salvation freely to all who receive Him as Saviour.

She taught them the very Word of God; and many of the girls, even the little ones, learned to recite, in their own language, the wonderful promise found in John 3:16: "For God so loved the world, that he gave his only begotten Son, that whosoever believeth in him should not perish, but have everlasting life."

DAVID LIVINGSTONE
MISSIONARY TO AFRICA

Story by Alice Bostrom

PRECIOUS PACKAGE

David rushed into his house. "Mother, come see what I've bought with my earnings," he called.

His mother held out her hands for the package. "What was so important that you had to spend your money?"

The Livingstone family had little money. Because of this, David had to go to work at the age of ten in a cotton mill, piecing together the threads on the spinning frames when the threads looked like they would break.

The boy worked from six in the morning until eight at night in the hot, stuffy Blantyre Mill. Most of his money went to the family, but this was his special package.

His mother opened it up and lifted out a book.

"Oh, David," she said, "was this what you wanted so much?" She held up a Latin book.

"Yes, Mother. I don't want to spend the rest of my life in the mill. I must get an education."

David's education began early when his father taught him to read and write. He went to school nights from eight to ten in the company school. Most children fell asleep after work, too tired to even play.

Mother put the book high on a shelf to keep it from the other children. She looked at him, "You do love to learn, don't you, son?"

"Yes, Mother, I do. And I love science. The next book I want to buy tells how to identify plants and herbs."

DECISION

David had given his life to Jesus as a boy. At age twenty he read a pamphlet from his church which changed his life.

It told of Charles Gutzlaff, a missionary to China. The words almost jumped off the page toward David. Gutzlaff was a new kind of missionary, a medical missionary.

Suddenly he realized, "I want to serve Jesus. I love science. I've always brought home plants and herbs and tried to identify them. I study rocks, birds, and trees. What if I could learn to be a doctor! I could heal the bodies and the hearts of the Chinese people." David told his parents of his decision.

"Mother, Father," he began, "I want to become a medical missionary!"

His parents looked both pleased and puzzled.

"David," his father said, "do you mean to study theology and medicine—to preach and doctor?"

"Yes, Father. Please read this pamphlet about Gutzlaff." He raced outside, fearing his parents' reaction. He thought about the years of study and the cost. God wanted him to go to the mission field. He knew God would provide a way.

Returning inside, David guessed from his parents' smiles they agreed with his decision. "Son," his father said, "you will have to work very hard. We have no money for college. But with God's help, you will go with our blessing."

THE DOORS TO CHINA CLOSE

David began attending Anderson College in Glasgow, Scotland. David's father gave him whatever money he could afford. The young man worked as a cotton spinner at the mill during his summer vacations from school to pay for his tuition and books.

He applied to the London Missionary Society for missionary training. David moved to London and lived at a boarding house while studying medicine.

"Good morning," said one of the other boarders. "My name is Robert Moffat."

"Good morning," replied David. "Are you the famous missionary from Africa?"

The man laughed. "I don't know how famous, but my mission station is Kuruman in South Africa."

The men talked together over meals. "We need a good doctor in Africa," said Mr. Moffat.

David smiled. "My heart is set on China."

He returned to his studies. Word came from the London Missionary Society, "David Livingstone has been accepted for training." He felt his heart pounding. "I will be a missionary to China!"

But soon thereafter his joy turned to sorrow. Britain and China went to war. No missionaries could go to China!

A PREACHER LIKE MOSES

David passed his examinations for the missionary society. Now he must learn to preach.

He lived with Joseph Moore, who was also preparing for the mission field. Together the young men studied Greek, Latin, and Hebrew.

Part of their studies was to prepare sermons and to submit them to Rev. Richard Cecil. After approval, they had to memorize the sermons and quote them in church.

David worked hard on his first sermon. He memorized the corrected version. Then an opportunity came. A pastor nearby became ill after his morning service.

This was David's chance! The people sent for him to preach during the evening service.

He stood at the pulpit. Slowly he read the Scripture passage. He opened his mouth to speak. Nothing came out. He couldn't remember the carefully prepared sermon.

"Friends, I have forgotten all I had to say," he apologized, running from the chapel.

He ran all the way home. Opening his Bible to the Book of Exodus, he read about a great Old Testament leader.

Moses couldn't preach. He had said to God, ". . . O my Lord, I am not eloquent, . . . but I am slow of speech, and of a slow tongue." David Livingstone, like Moses, had to depend on God's promise, "Now therefore go, and I will be with thy mouth, and teach thee what thou shalt say." (Exodus 4:12)

VOYAGE OUT

Since David could not go to China, he decided, with the approval of the mission society, to go to Africa.

He passed the medical licensing exams in the fall of 1840 and became a physician at the age of twenty-seven.

The family arose at 5 o'clock on the morning of November 17. Mrs. Livingstone made coffee.

"I'll read the Scripture this morning," said David. He read Psalms 121 and 135 and prayed.

"Come on, son," his parents said. "We'll walk to Glasgow with you and wait until you board the Liverpool steamer."

Three days later, David was ordained in Albion Chapel, London, as a missionary. Reverend Cecil conducted the service. Despite David's first failure at preaching, he was now ready to be a missionary.

On December 8, 1840, David boarded the ship *George* and sailed for Africa.

The ship's captain spoke to David, "You seem curious about everything aboard the ship."

"I am, Captain Donaldson," replied David.

"Would you like to learn to use the quadrant and to steer the ship by the stars?"

"I would, sir, very much."

"Meet me on deck just before midnight."

David began his training in the use of the quadrant, lunar observation, and determining positions by the stars.

RHINOCEROS DINNER

After a stormy voyage, the *George* landed at the Cape on the southern tip of Africa.

From Port Elizabeth, David traveled more than seven hundred miles to Kuruman, in what is now Botswana. The trip took three months by oxcart.

Robert Moffat and his family remained in England. David had hoped to spend time with Mr. Moffat in Kuruman.

David decided to leave, to spend time away from the English-speaking people, and to concentrate on learning the local languages. Four native men went with him.

People rushed from village to village shouting, "The doctor is coming! The doctor is coming!" Sick people came from as far away as 200 miles to meet the white doctor in his tent. They hoped he would heal them.

David wrote a letter home to Scotland saying, "We boiled rhinoceros, which was tough. The meat was our supper. Porridge made of Indian corn meal and gravy of the meat made a very good dinner the next day."

David learned the people's languages as he sewed up their wounds, dressed the cuts, set broken limbs, and treated them for dysentery. While he traveled, he looked for a new place where he could begin his mission work.

DAVID IN THE LION'S JAWS

David moved to a new village, called Mabotsa, to start his missionary effort. Lions often came to the village, sneaking into the cattle pens at night to kill the animals. They destroyed nine sheep and goats in one day.

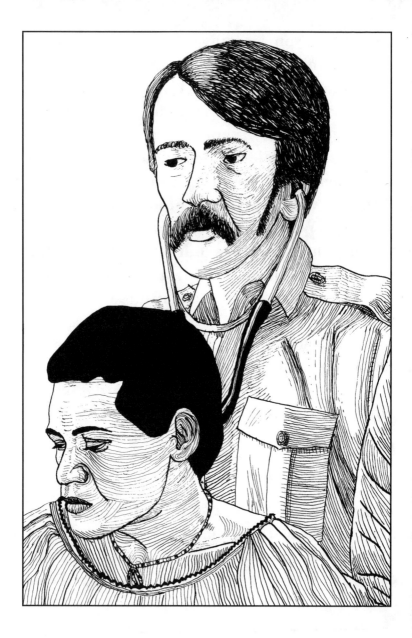

The villagers circled and threatened one lion. David hoped the people would kill one lion so that the others would leave the area.

Mebalwe, a native school teacher, shot at the lion and missed. The animal broke free. David shot both barrels and saw the lion's tail stand erect in anger.

"Stop a little, till I load again!" he shouted. He put the bullets into the rifle.

Someone yelled, "Look out!"

Suddenly, out of the bushes the lion lunged at David. The mighty jaws crunched down on his shoulder, tearing his flesh and crushing his bone. The lion fell heavily on him.

David heard the lion's fierce roar. He was too shocked by the blow to speak. Mebalwe stood thirty feet away and shot. The gun misfired. The lion roared at Mebalwe and sunk his teeth into the flesh of his thigh.

A third man rushed at the lion with a spear. The animal caught the man's shoulder. At that moment the earlier gunshots took effect. The lion fell dead.

RECOVERY AT KURUMAN

David recovered slowly from his broken shoulder. The lion left eleven teeth marks on his arm. As the three men regained their health, David said, "Praise God Who delivered me from so great a danger. I hope I shall never forget God's mercy."

Because David was the only doctor at Mabotsa, his friends took him back to Kuruman for help. The Moffats had returned from England.

Robert Moffat called his eldest daughter, Mary. "David Livingstone's been hurt by a lion. Will you nurse him?"

"Of course, Father."

David watched Mary while he recovered. She was a kind, gentle nurse and a fine Christian.

Slowly he could spend more time outside. There he observed Mary as she taught a class of sixty children. Each child looked at Mary with respect. She could speak the native language better than David. She was, after all, a missionary's daughter, and she had lived most of her life in Africa.

Mary noticed David's constant watching. As they walked one day, she said, "David, I feel your eyes follow me all day long."

"Mary, I love you," he confessed. He worked up his courage to ask her to become his wife.

She consented, and her parents gave their approval.

TO THE RESCUE

Although slavery had ended in England, it had not ended in Africa.

As David traveled about 150 miles from his mission home, he stopped his wagon near where a girl of eleven sat.

"Who are you and what are you doing here?" asked David.

The girl shook with fear. According to the custom of her country, she should not speak to men. Finally, she spoke.

"I lived with my sister in another village. Now she is dead. Take me to your home, or they will sell me as a slave."

"We will protect you," said both David and a native Christian, helping her into the wagon.

A man with a gun approached. "Give me the girl," he demanded. "She's mine."

"Listen to me," the Christian spoke up. "I am the son of a chief. You can't have her."

The man raised the gun. "She belongs to me. Get her."

David walked to the wagon. He put many strings of beads around her neck and brought her forward.

"Look at those beads," said the man with the gun.

"If you want the beads, we might trade them for the girl," David said.

The girl stood again, shaking in fear for her life.

"I want all the beads," the man said.

"Take them and go," said David.

He hid the girl in the wagon so no one could find her.

MA ROBERT

Mary's life changed at Mabotsa. She helped teach the children reading, writing, and Bible stories. She laughed as the other teacher,

Mebalwe, taught the alphabet by singing it to the tune of "Auld Lang Syne."

She gathered the women around her to teach them Bible stories.

"I'm so busy all the time, David," she said.

"You're such a wonderful help here, Mary. But we must prepare to move to a new missionary home in Chonuane."

Mary helped pack their belongings. At Chonuane, the Livingstones' first child was born. They called him Robert Moffat Livingstone, for Mary's father.

David smiled at his wife. "You now have a new name!" he said.

"Yes, David. Now I am Ma Robert."

The people called her "Ma," meaning "mother of," and "Robert" for her first-born son. Later in his travels David named his boat for Mary. He called it the *MA ROBERT*.

Ma Robert's day began at 6 a.m. She baked bread for the family in an oven made in an ant hill, made their clothes and soap, dipped candles, looked after the baby, and taught school. Her day ended with a prayer meeting at 9 p.m.

DANGER IN THE WOODS

The black rhinoceros was one of the most dangerous animals in Africa. A hunting party encountered one during a trip near David's home. The rhinoceros charged at the wagon driver and gored his stomach.

"Someone must go and get Dr. Livingstone!" a hunter shouted.

The messenger ran all the way to David's home, arriving after dark.

"Dr. Livingstone, will you come?" he said. "A rhinoceros horn gored our wagon driver."

"Yes, I'll get my bag," David said. He began to load the medicines.

David's friends were afraid. "You cannot go ten miles through the woods at night," said one friend.

"No. You must not go!" said another. "It is certain death."

David smiled at his friends. "I appreciate your concern. God will protect me."

He mounted his horse and rode through the woods.

He had no difficulty on the journey.

David arrived too late. The man could not be saved. Again David returned through the woods, trusting his safety to God.

SECHELE

The Bakwain people became the center of David's work in Chonuane. Their chief, Sechele, showed interest in the Bible message. He wanted to understand.

David taught Sechele to read.

"Now, give me a book," said Sechele.

David gave him a New Testament in his own language. He loved to read and wanted the Bakwains to believe God's Word.

"If you want," Sechele said, "I'll call my head men. We'll use rhinoceros whips and make all the people believe."

"No," said David. "God wants true Believers, not people who are forced to believe."

The Bakwain people and Chief Sechele moved to the village of Kolobeng. David, Mary, Robert, and baby Agnes moved with them. Thomas Livingstone, a third child, was born at Kolobeng.

The chief wanted to build "a house for God" and pay for it himself. He employed two hundred men to construct the building.

Sechele told David of other tribes beyond the Kalahari Desert who needed to hear God's Word. He offered to lead David to the Makololo tribe, which no other European had ever visited. That trip led to Lake Ngami, one of many beautiful sights in Africa, which David was the first European to see.

BOER RAID

David continued to fight against slavery. He paid the people who worked for him and could not understand the Boers, nearby farmers, who insisted on keeping slaves.

The Boers complained about David to the London Missionary Society, with no results. When that failed, they threatened to kill David.

He believed that Mary and his children were no longer safe in Africa. Reluctantly, he took them to the Cape and put them aboard a ship bound for England.

David's heart ached at the loss of Mary and the children. He took the long wagon trip home to Kolobeng.

The missionary reached home soon after the Boers had attacked the place. He found the sofa, table, bed, dishes, desk, and iron chairs gone, and the wooden chairs broken. He could not believe the sight of his books, which he had loved all his life, torn apart and dumped in a pile. All the medicine bottles and windows had been smashed. This meant the Boers did not want him to practice medicine in Kolobeng. He knew he could not rebuild or live in the house without his tools, food, and cattle.

David kneeled and prayed, "Thank You, God, for protecting Mary and the children. Show me where You want me to serve."

A WATERFALL FOR A QUEEN

No roads crossed Africa. David set out again, searching for a way across the continent. If such a way could be opened, missionaries could easily get into the interior.

David believed God had sent him to Africa to preach, to heal, to translate, and to open the way for future missionaries.

His hope was that transportation across the continent might someday be by water. With this in mind, he chose a route to the interior along the Zambesi River.

Throughout the long journey, he wrote in his journal, making maps of the area. Each clear night he made sightings of the stars to determine his location, just as he had learned to do at sea.

The great Zambesi became a rushing roar as he and his men got closer to a mighty waterfall. Water sprayed hundreds of feet into the air as it crashed 320 feet to the canyon beneath. Columns of mist rose from the zigzag river below.

"This must be like Niagara Falls in America," said David. He measured the distance with his eyes. "It must be even greater! I will call it Victoria Falls for our queen!"

VISIT FROM STANLEY

Livingstone received many awards from Queen Victoria for his discoveries and from scientific societies for his contributions in geography, astronomy, and other sciences.

People in America wanted to know more about David. This interest made the *New York Herald* send reporter Henry Stanley to Africa to find the missionary and write his story.

David knew nothing about the search. He had received no word from Europe or his family in two years.

Stanley organized an expedition in Zanzibar. One hundred ninety-two persons started in five caravans to find one missionary doctor.

Eight months later, David's men came running and shouting, "A white man is coming!"

A man carrying an American flag led the caravan. Behind him, men carried bales of cloth, tin bath tubs, huge kettles, cooking pots, and tents. The two men faced each other: David, surprised to see this stranger, and Stanley, relieved to find the tired, pale man wearing the familiar blue cap with gold braid.

"Dr. Livingstone, I presume?"

"Yes," he said and raised the cap in greeting. They clasped hands.

"I thank God, Doctor, I have been permitted to see you," said Stanley.

"I feel thankful that I am here to welcome you!"

Stanley brought the news of the world and the mail from Livingstone's family and friends in England. His good food helped David recover his strength. "You have brought me new life," David said.

David Livingstone traveled 29,000 miles in Africa over a thirty-year period. He was the first man other than native Africans to see Lake Ngami, Lake Shirwa, Lake Nyassa, Lake Moero, Lake Bangweolo, the Zambesi River, and Victoria Falls. The city of Livingstone, Zambia, located near Victoria Falls, has a museum dedicated to him which contains his journals and many other personal items.

The great missionary/doctor/explorer died near Lake Bangweolo, in Africa, on April 30, 1873, and was later buried in England. His greatest joy came from serving God faithfully throughout his life.